Puppetry,
Theatre and
Arts Education

Puppetry in Theatre and Arts Education

Head, Hands and Heart

Johanna Smith

methuen | drama

LONDON • NEW YORK • OXFORD • NEW DELHI • SYDNEY

METHUEN DRAMA
Bloomsbury Publishing Plc
50 Bedford Square, London, WC1B 3DP, UK
1385 Broadway, New York, NY 10018, USA

BLOOMSBURY, METHUEN DRAMA and the Methuen Drama
logo are trademarks of Bloomsbury Publishing Plc

First published in Great Britain 2019

A catalogue record for this book is available from the British Library.

Library of Congress Cataloging-in-Publication Data
Names: Smith, Johanna, 1972- author.
Title: Puppetry in theatre and arts education : head, hands and heart /
Johanna Smith.
Description: London, UK ; New York, NY : Methuen Drama, 2019. |
Includes bibliographical references.
Identifiers: LCCN 2018025923 | ISBN 9781350012905 (hbk.) |
ISBN 9781350012912 (pbk.) |
ISBN 9781350012899 (ePDF) | ISBN 9781350012929 (ebk.)
Subjects: LCSH: Puppet theater in education.
Classification: LCC PN1979.E4 S65 2019 | DDC 791.5/3–dc23
LC record available at https://lccn.loc.gov/2018025923

ISBN:	HB:	978-1-350-01290-5
	PB:	978-1-350-01291-2
	ePDF:	978-1-350-01289-9
	eBook:	978-1-350-01292-9

Typeset by Integra Software Services Pvt. Ltd.
Printed and bound in India

To find out more about our authors and books visit www.bloomsbury.com
and sign up for our newsletters.

Contents

List of Figures

List of Tables

Acknowledgments

This book would not be possible without the help and inspiration of the "puppet people" in my life, particularly Gina Pavlova, Elena Velasco, Miss Linda Dryden, Johnny Saldaña, Tim Lagasse, Paul Zaloom, Clare Dolan, and all the folks from Bread and Puppet, Eric Bass, and everyone at Sandglass, and the many amazing folks I've met at the O'Neill Puppetry Conference. Thank you to the members of the American Alliance for Theatre & Education who have supported and featured my work at conferences for years. Big huge thanks to my colleagues at CSUSB Theatre who have made all of this madness possible (especially Margaret Perry who first encouraged me to create my puppetry class) and to my daughter Katya, my collaborator and photographer (she took all the good ones).

1 Introduction

Why write this book?

There are lots of wonderful books available about puppets and puppet making within educational settings. You can find many of them by contacting puppetry organizations such as UNIMA (the International Association of Puppetry, which is a wonderful group), Puppeteers of America, or your local puppetry guild. It took many years of working with children before I had something to add to the conversation about puppetry education, which has been rich and thorough for a long time. Most puppetry books are craft oriented and describe how to make a variety of puppets. They provide patterns, scripts, and fun activities. Some share ways to use the art of puppetry to explore global traditions and cultures. The best texts include developmental information for educators and strategies for varied populations. All of these books are great resources and I encourage you to find and use them.

However, public school education has radically changed since the publication of most educational puppetry texts. It's time to reintroduce puppetry to a new generation of educators (and artists) so that it becomes accessible to a new generation of children. Several reasons teachers repeatedly provide for not using puppets in an educational setting are that they feel they are not "crafty" or "artistic" enough to make puppets; there is not enough time to make puppets in the school day; it's not "educational enough" for administrators; or they are intimidated by how beautiful professional puppets look and feel their work will never compare. What educators need to understand is that the educational power of puppetry lies in its process, not the products. You don't need a lot of fancy, expensive materials or a formal puppet show performance. In fact, sometimes the less "fancy stuff" you use and the less pressure there is to perform, the more powerful the discoveries tend to be.

How can this be? It's all how you look at things! In education, thanks to the work of Wiggins and McTighe in *Understanding by Design* (2005), we've learned to ask complex questions that encourage children to experiment, fail, try again, discover, debate, critique, revise, and (hopefully) deeply understand something. Wiggins and McTighe's "backwards design" method is a perfect tool for developing young minds and is the inspiration for my process in this book. So, instead of spending a lot of time on what puppets are and how to make them (which has been done so well for so long), let's take a step back and really look at why we use puppets in education. What's so special about them? What makes them different from any other art form? Why are children so fascinated by them? How can we use their inherent power to draw students in? What else can puppets teach? How can students discover these things for themselves? How can we inspire passion for learning more about something wonderful?

To sum up, this text is intended to provide teachers, puppeteers, and theatre professionals with a step-by-step approach to teaching the essential concepts inherent in puppetry to all types of students. This is not a prescriptive series that must be followed exactly and in order, rather, it is a set of concepts that, if explored, will enhance any visual or performing arts lesson or puppet performance you want to create. You'll find that some of the deep learning that takes place will enrich students' lives holistically; often in unpredictable ways. Embrace a little chaos and join in yourself! Please modify these ideas to suit your interests and the populations you teach.

Why should innovative educators use puppetry in the classroom?

Puppetry is the art form that combines all the others. Puppeteers must master visual art, dance/movement, music, and all the jobs in theatre (director, designer, actor, lighting and sound design, writer, and now filmmaker). Puppetry can be used with all ages and populations, and has been found to be particularly effective with students with special needs. In a world where funding for arts education is a precious and tenuous thing, puppetry can be used to address many arts with all students with fewer resources. Puppetry may be especially useful for educators who must address all of the fine arts in standards-based practice, yet are limited in time.

However, there's a fundamental element of puppetry that can address a great need in today's classrooms. It seems that the dominant forces are pushing for students to have skills in the *virtual* world of computers and technology. It's becoming clear that we can't neglect the importance of developing skills for the *actual* world. Let's explore and celebrate the "tinkering" of our ancestors and the craft traditions that have been a source of pride for all human cultures. Let's join the wave of "Makers" who are embracing both technology and old-fashioned crafts in their work. We need to encourage the acquisition of *tactile* skills and familiarity with materials and their properties. I like to think of this as an aspect of "manual intelligence," or "hand smarts," as coined by Frank R. Wilson in *The Hand: How its use shapes the brain, language, and human culture* (1999). As Wilson says, "How does, or should, the education system accommodate the fact that the hand is not merely a metaphor or an icon for humanness, but often the real-life focal point—the lever or the launching pad—of a successful and genuinely fulfilling life?" (1999, 14).

Flexible, creative thinkers and makers will create the innovations we need in a world of scarce resources. I want my students to be the ones who see creative potential where most people see waste. I want my students to see the potential in every object and every person. If students develop advanced practical skills, research is beginning to show they will be *happier*. Why not place a premium on fostering joy and fun in our classrooms? We need to teach young people to love discovery and learning, and puppetry is a great way to do it.

How do I advocate for and explain this unusual approach to pedagogy to my administrators?

I have found that the best arguments for using puppetry-based teaching methods are almost exactly like the arguments used for using the arts in the classroom, particularly theatre. Advocacy organizations for arts education will be able to direct you to a number of excellent resources that use current research to explain why drama works so well. Thanks to new technologies we are now able to analyze exactly how the human mind learns (although there is still quite a lot to discover). We can share the tools of advocacy from all other art forms, but it is also important to define how puppetry has particular strengths that are not found in any other discipline. We can find connections with puppetry in all four fine arts: dance, theatre, music, and visual arts.

The core of dance education is developing movement literacy, body awareness, and interpreting concepts by applying the elements of dance in choreography. Theatre uses movement to activate characters and abstract ideas. Movement skills are deeply tied to cognitive development. In other words, we can't separate the physical body from the mind when considering the learning process:

> There is a growing commitment to the idea that the mind
> must be understood in the context of its relationship to a

physical body that interacts with the world ... Hence human cognition, rather than being centralized, abstract, and sharply distinct from peripheral input and output modules may instead have deep roots in sensorimotor processing. (Wilson 2002, 625)

Puppetry is defined by movement as well. A puppet that doesn't move is just a statue or doll. Like dance, when moving puppets we activate the body as a fundamental part of learning.

Drama explores the creation of entire worlds. Students take on roles and use their imaginations to view the world "as if" they are another person. They modify their voices to create characters and express emotions. The core of drama education is developing empathy in students. Like dance, drama engages more of the senses and becomes a more concrete experience for learners:

Education through drama removes a traditional learning block of academic routine structure and brings learning into a physical realm that can be acted out to be made real to the students. More senses are activated compared to the absorption of knowledge in a classroom. The belief here is that when new knowledge is generated from within an authentic milieu, learning is viewed as more genuine, dynamic, and meaningful. (Hough and Hough 2012, 456)

Like drama, puppetry is often about creating characters. Students engage in incredibly complex cognitive processes, for example, when performing improvisations between puppet characters.

What distinguishes puppetry from dance and drama is the addition of the transformed, active object (and I'm including the transformed body as object, for example, if you draw eyes on your hand it's then a puppet object). Movement and character are invoked through the transformation of one thing into another "creature," with its own view of the world. In addition, the puppet is often an object that must be constructed or created. Its maker must solve the problem of how its construction influences its movement. This process can be discovered organically, or the builder has to engineer a solution. Both are cognitively rich learning experiences.

Visual arts (and theatre design) and music specifically connect the use of the hand to learning, or as Wilson states, "The hand speaks to the brain as surely as the brain speaks to the hand" (1999, 59). The creation and mastery of musical instruments and artistic tools for intricate use by the hand might have even developed human brains:

> There is growing evidence that H. sapiens acquired in its new hand not simply the mechanical capacity for refined manipulative and tool-using skills, but, as time passed and events unfolded, an impetus to the redesign, or reallocation, of the brain's circuitry. (Wilson 1999, 59)

By building and manipulating puppets, students use tools and create real objects that are manipulated by the hands. Mastery is difficult and takes practice, much like learning to play a violin:

> We are now at a point where we can more fully sense the convergence of the neurologic, linguistic, developmental, and anthropologic perspectives in our search for an understanding of the role of the hand in human life. This merged perspective prepares us to examine more closely the role of the hand within contemporary social and cultural contexts. More particularly, it prepares us to consider how we do, or how we might, develop our own unseen, dormant, knowing, praxic, inventive hand and put it to our own personal and expressive use—to make it speak, and ourselves more articulate. (Wilson 1999, 209)

Finally, by sharing aspects of all the other art forms, puppetry integrates the arts. This can be powerful (and, quite frankly, time and cost effective). Educators are moving toward the interconnection of disciplines as a powerful methodology. "Transdisciplinarity" and "Arts Integration" are important topics to explore in relation to puppetry:

> *With new standards and initiatives, general education has shifted its priorities from rote learning of academic content to understanding overarching concepts and building thinking skills that underlie all disciplines ... This change in focus toward conceptual and procedural skills should prompt general educators to entertain alternative pedagogies that foster these abilities ... Indeed, this may be an opportunity to rethink education as a whole, to shape a new paradigm of education built on a more dynamic, creative, organic, and realistic vision of how the world works, how young people learn, and how the mind understands its experience and the world. ...*
>
> *While knowledge in an academic discipline is important, the focus for art integrators is on how that knowledge is acquired and how deeply it is understood ... Similarly, in art integration, learners explore knowledge and perspectives of the academic disciplines while using artistic and integrated methods that disrupt conventional discipline-specific habits of mind. For instance, learners in an art-integrated classroom often play with and visualize ideas in novel and aesthetic ways that are foreign to academic practices. (Marshall 2014, 105, 107)*

So, in short, if someone asks you why you use puppets in your classroom, you can tell them you are engaging sensorimotor processing to develop human cognition, generating knowledge from within an authentic milieu, developing empathy in your students, fostering brain development through the use of the hand, and integrating the arts in a transdisciplinary curriculum.

ABOUT MY LESSON PLAN STRUCTURE

How are these lesson plans put together?

The basic structure of my lesson plans is based on a tried-and-true structure from the field of creative drama. I first learned the lesson plan appproach of pique, plan, play, and evaluate from the American founder of creative drama, Winifred Ward, and grew to rely on the very similar motivation, presentation, construction, playing, and assessment puppetry lesson plan structure that I learned from my mentor Johnny Saldaña. I've taken that basic structure and added some ideas from *Understanding by Design* by Wiggins and McTighe. There's quite a bit of similarity between their lesson planning approach and drama education. For example, their concept of starting with a "hook" to draw students into the lesson is the same "motivation" drama teachers use every day. The biggest influence of *Understanding by Design* on my structure is the use of a "big question" (which they call an essential question or essential understanding) to guide and frame the lesson. Here is what you'll see for each lesson that explores puppetry as a fine art.

Suggested age range

Some of these lessons are possible to do with all ages and some require more advanced social and cognitive abilities. I'll give you an estimate of the ages that, in my experience, respond well to these lessons. Please feel free to modify things to suit your students. I always tell teachers that they know their students best.

Time needed

Lessons can range from thirty minutes to a long unit, with plenty of flexibility. Suggestions are included for cutting things short or digging more deeply.

The big questions

These are questions you can ask and re-ask throughout the lesson. The students' answers should change as they make discoveries. You can really track how their understanding deepens over time. I like to post the questions very prominently in the room as we explore each one.

Materials/preparation

As I tell my pre-teaching students, "Your memory works really well now. Take advantage of it. It may not always be there for you when you're teaching." I learned to create very detailed lists of what to have ready so I don't forget something crucial. Don't forget to take a moment to update this section if you modify a lesson plan.

Boundaries and safety

My assumption is that teachers will know to go over proper use of materials and tools and expected classroom behavior norms in advance. If there are specific rules for appropriate use of materials or a need for caution I will point them out.

Assessment strategies

I like to think of my assessment strategies well before I teach a lesson. I use lots of tools for direct assessment of activities (which are included here), but I feel teacher observations are the most important tool we have to gauge student learning. Look for the "Aha!" moments, listen for the "Wows!" Savor the times you hear "Teacher, look at this!" Better yet, ask caregivers if your students continued their puppetry explorations at home. That is the best proof that our students are applying what they learn independently. All lessons benefit from a structured performance/critique process. That process builds critical thinking skills and helps communicate the important role students have when they are the audience.

Figure 1 Sock rock star puppet.

Opening/hook

How will you get students excited about the lesson? Granted, the fact that you're doing puppetry is already a great motivator, so this should be easy! I've included some approaches that have worked well for me over the years as a performer and artist-in-schools.

Figure 2 Children with their various puppets.

Planning

How will you set up groups or prepare the space for what you need? Where/How are you constructing or performing? How can the students help with materials? Do you need to go over safety rules? Do the students need any information to be successful? Do the students have any questions before you begin? Each lesson has content and a few planning tips that have helped me in classrooms.

Tasks

I provide clear instructions that you can read to the students for all puppet tasks. You can also hand out written instructions for reference. I am always surprised to see how much clear instructions help students work efficiently and independently.

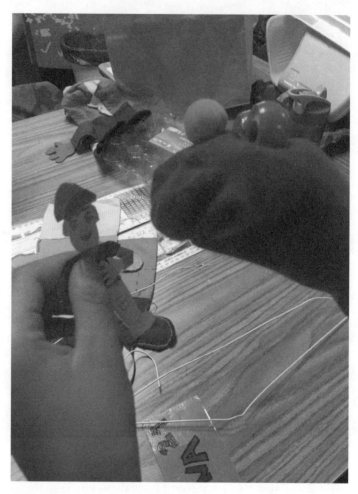

Figure 3 A paper puppet and a sock puppet.

Sharing effective work

The critique process is a fantastic assessment tool for any of the fine arts. When an artist hears a response from others about their creation, they learn to think critically about their work, and the commenters learn to describe their personal observations and responses. In my puppetry courses, I try to ensure that this process of giving and receiving feedback is very positive and constructive.

This is because I feel the puppetry classroom is one place where students should feel supported, safe, and free to create. Often, their experiences with the arts and critique have been negative and discouraging. That doesn't mean you can't point out when a puppet doesn't clearly tell the story or if students are not doing their best work. It means thought is given to the process of feedback so the environment stays welcoming for all. One big ground rule in my classes is "compare and despair." Students should be talking about their own work and not comparing it to others' efforts. This can be very difficult for young people, so model your delight in how they solved the problems you gave them, and focus less on the aesthetics of the object created. Be kind to yourself when sharing your own work too, as this sets an important example.

When I have students share, they each present their work to the class. The rest of the class is invited to share what was effective in the work, or simply to describe what they saw and heard. When evaluating work as the teacher, be as descriptive and affirmative as possible. In other words, affirm the choices they made that solved the problem at hand and validate their artistic work. Then, the performers/makers are invited to respond with their intentions and any surprises they found in the feedback. Then, everyone (including the instructor) is invited to share "What ifs." These are one-sentence suggestions for improvement that start with the words "What if." The presenters can collect some "What ifs" and address them in further rehearsals. If you see evidence of improvement, it tells you very clearly that the students were able to receive and integrate feedback into their work. That is a powerful assessment tool that is unique to the arts.

Reflections, connections, and next directions

Whenever possible, I provide ideas for further exploration and some prompts to help students reflect on what they've learned and what they want to know more about.

A note on lesson planning for young children

I use a slightly different approach for interdisciplinary classroom lessons that is similar to creative drama in its use of puppet making and puppet manipulation as teaching tools. I use the term "puppetizing" to describe this approach, as coined by Tamra Hunt and Nancy Renfro in *Puppetry in Early Childhood Education* (1982). For these plans I add educational goals and more structure for activities.

A note on student quality work

You may notice as you read through these ideas that I don't often provide elaborate templates or strict, step-by-step instructions. I also use found materials as much as possible. There's a very good reason for that. The fun of puppetry (and the strongest learning) takes place when students are solving a problem for themselves, or even better *discovering* the problems in the first place. If they were merely coloring and cutting out a pattern or using premade "perfect" materials, they wouldn't be flexing nearly as many "cognitive muscles." However, as a result the puppets they create will often not look "slick" or "professional" to many people. But that's the point—students need to do things on their own in order to learn the actual skills they will need as adults. It shouldn't be easy—it should be theirs. Students should be free to create and not worry about wasting expensive materials. If they make a mistake, have plenty of materials around to encourage them to try again as many times as they need to. Let them find out that mistakes are part of the learning process.

After each puppetry lesson, the puppets should be in a state of beautiful decay, which is proof that they have served their purposes well. Make sure to let students take puppets home to play with and share with loved ones after lessons are done.

2 Johanna's Newspaper Challenge

Or The Puppetry Test

Introduction

If you are going to do several of the lessons from this collection, please consider treating them as a "unit" and take the opportunity to assess your students' overall growth in puppetry skills. Assessment of creative and collaborative arts activities can be tricky. Here in the United States, education policies are constantly changing, and sometimes rather radically. As I write this, the standards I used for this project are about to be replaced with new ones. It's difficult to determine specific, measurable learning outcomes with an open-ended arts-based lesson when you are not exactly sure what students will come up with or what will happen. Besides, if you have to "test" students, doesn't that make everything less fun? Will it not add stress to your hard-won creative environment? Not necessarily! Believe it or not, coming up with assessment tasks can be a creative and fun thing for an educator and their students.

Originally developed for the Coyote Conservatory Summer Puppetry Program, funded by a grant from the National Endowment for the Arts, San Bernardino, California, in 2007.

As the expert of your classroom, you know your students better than a distant policy maker. You are the best person to identify what your students need. Usually, it is possible to find the key ideas within a given standard. Then, develop a "performance task" that you can do twice: a "pretest" before the lesson really begins, and then a "posttest" at the end of instruction after they have gained knowledge and skills. Changes in student performance of the same task can clearly show you changes in their understanding.

How do you come up with a task like that and make it engaging for students? Fundamentally, you need to identify what students should understand and what they can do to show you they understand it. I also like to think about what I would enjoy watching my students accomplish. I am the type of learner who needs examples, so I thought I would go through my process of developing a major assessment for a summer program I created for the National Endowment for the Arts in 2007. I think it works well as an overall indicator of student learning. It is also based on a tried-and-true puppet-making technique that has been featured at puppetry conferences for years—the newspaper puppet.

To start, I selected the standards for theatre in Table 1 from the California Visual and Performing Arts Challenge Standards. They are fairly broad and contain lots of room for different approaches.

It is almost impossible to cover everything in each of those standards in one task, but they contain the two most important ideas I wanted to assess: can puppetry teach students to collaborate, and is it possible to assess the group design of a puppet made of very simple elements? For standard 2.1, I narrowed down my focus and rewrote a more specific goal: "Students participate in cooperative improvisations." When several students have to operate one puppet and make it come to life, it is clearly a task that requires collaboration to succeed. For

Table 1 Standards for theatre chosen from the California Visual and Performing Arts Challenge Standards

National or State	Standard Number	Standard Description
CA–Theatre	2.1 (grade 3)	Participate in cooperative script writing or improvisations that incorporate the Five Ws.
CA–Theatre	2.3 (grade 4)	Design or create costumes, props, makeup, or masks to communicate a character in formal or informal performances.

Johanna's Newspaper Challenge

Materials/preparation

For each group at least :

- two newspapers;
- one roll of masking tape;
- a small ball of yarn or string;
- one pair of scissors (to be used only to cut the yarn);
- a camera for documentation (if available).

Assessment strategies

By observing the informal sharing process you should be able to gain all the evidence necessary to determine if the students can collaborate. You should also see variations in understanding or mastery. To make life easier (and fair), tools such as rubrics can help an educator articulate exactly what they saw and what it means in terms of student learning. Table 2 shows the rubric I have developed for this task, which has grown and changed as I have worked with more and more students. In particular, I have a better understanding of what student work tends to look like at different levels of mastery and understanding. Rubrics also show changes in your understanding as an educator.

Table 2 Rubric for Johanna's Newspaper Challenge

Standard	4—Advanced	3—Proficient	2—Basic	1—Below Basic
CA–Theatre 2.1 (grade 3) Collaboration	All team members function peacefully and efficiently within the time period given to complete the task of building a newspaper puppet. Students effectively communicate ideas and use members' strengths.	Most team members are actively involved in building. The balance in the group is skewed—some members contribute less. A usable puppet is created within the time limit.	The group has trouble getting started and does not finish their puppet. There are minor conflicts in the group. The group is able to work with what they have after the time limit but the puppet is not complete.	No team members are able to cooperate. The task is not complete and no puppet is created, even given extra time.
CA–Theatre 2.1 (grade 3) Improvisation	All team members listen, respond, and initiate within the improvisation to create the illusion of life within the puppet. Students are able to give and take leadership. Each student initiates movements that the other group members follow (or enhances initiated movements in creative ways), leading to discoveries in performance.	Most team member are actively involved in manipulating the puppet. The balance in the group is skewed—one group member heavily dominates. The illusion of life is maintained most of the time and the movement tasks are completed.	The team has to resort to speaking often to manipulate the puppet. There are few moments where the illusion of life is created. Some movement tasks are not completed.	Team members do not listen to each other nor work together. The puppet is not manipulated
CA–Theatre 2.3 (grade 4) Character	One character's unique and surprising point of view is clearly communicated in the informal performance. The group "knows" what the puppet should do next and can organically make it happen without talking.	One character's point of view is evident. The movement is not completely smooth (for example, the group is dominated by one puppeteer). There are some moments where it's not clear what's happening.	The group resorts to a lot of talking in order to communicate to create the movement. It is not often clear what the character is doing.	There is no character created. The informal performance does not occur.
CA–Theatre 2.3 (grade 4) Design	All team members contribute ideas and support in designing and making the puppet. The puppet goes beyond the human form (or is a very clever variation of a human, for example, one that can transform).	Most team members are fully involved in designing and making the puppet. The puppet has a distinct and chosen form.	The design and construction of the puppet is unbalanced (not a clear form).	There is no group effort in designing the puppet, leading to conflict within the group and an inability to make a usable puppet.

standard 2.3, my shortened version is "Students design a puppet to communicate a character in an informal performance." This is a clear statement of a task students can do. I can now combine these two more specific goals into one "challenge" activity. Can students build a puppet out of newspaper and manipulate that puppet as a team? Can multiple puppeteers cooperate to create the illusion of one living creature?

The fun part about this challenge is not revealing much information to the students at all—just provide the materials for them and these instructions. Time them strictly and do not provide any assistance beyond answering simple procedural or clarifying questions.

Using this information, you can let parents and caregivers know how students are progressing with very specific skills. As a parent myself, I would be very interested to know if my child's collaboration skills were improving, for example. The skills we teach using puppetry and all of the arts are often incredibly important for success and happiness in life.

Make sure to do this challenge at the beginning of your exploration of puppetry in your classroom, and again at the conclusion. What changes and what can we learn from it?

Task 1: Puppet making

You must collaborate in teams of three to four to construct one puppet. You may only use newspaper, masking tape (small pieces only), and yarn (only for manipulation, not decoration). The time limit for building is thirty minutes.

Task 2: Improvisation

Everyone in the group must work together to manipulate the puppet and improvise a sixty-second scene. The puppet must walk, sit down, breathe, get back up, improvise something you feel it "wants" to do, and walk away. (Optional: Your improvisation will be recorded and you will get a chance to watch it.)

Sharing effective work

After this activity I like to have a brainstorming session with students. Using the prompt "What is good puppetry?" list the things that make a puppetry performance effective and believable. I find it interesting to post this list in the classroom for students to refer to and update as they get new ideas.

Some things students have come up with over the years for what makes good puppeteers that I've enjoyed are:

- Work together
- Focus on the puppet
- Surprise the audience
- Are an ensemble
- Have fun
- Follow the puppet's center
- Share a brain!

Reflections, connections, and next directions

Ask your students the following questions at the start of your puppetry unit and again at the end. Post these questions in your classroom during the unit. How do their answers change and what does that show you about their understanding of puppetry?

1 What is a puppet?
2 What kind of puppets are there?

3 Who is a puppeteer and what do they do?

4 What is good puppetry?

5 Why do people watch puppet shows? (This one is optional and more advanced.)

3 **What is a Puppet?**

The Plastic Bags Lesson

Suggested age range

Eight to adult.

Time needed

At least sixty minutes. Can be broken up into shorter sessions.

The big questions

How do puppeteers collaborate to create the illusion of life? What can puppets do that people can't?

Materials/preparation

Whiteboard, chart paper, or chalkboard for brainstorming.
"Eyeballs" puppet for the teacher (see Figures 4 and 5).
Plastic grocery bags or small plastic trash bags, any color, try to find at least two per student.
Long tables cleared of all stuff and all chairs.
A way to play some fun music (preferably without lyrics).

Assessment strategies

Checklist provided for informal performance.

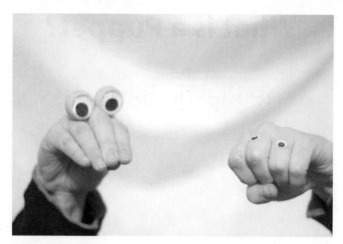

Figure 4 Eyeball hand puppets.

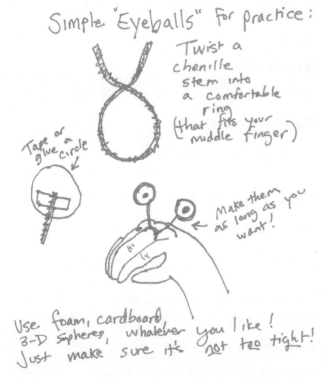

Simple "Eyeballs" for practice:

Twist a chenille stem into a comfortable ring (that fits your middle finger)

Tape or glue a circle ←

Make them as long as you want! ←

Use foam, cardboard, 3-D spheres, whatever you like! Just make sure it's not too tight!

Figure 5 Simple eyeballs.

Opening/hook

Transformation game: Have students sit in a circle as they are able. Pass one empty plastic bag around the group. Each student needs to create something with the plastic bag. Anything that *isn't* a bag is acceptable. After going around the group, if the students haven't made something like a puppet, I take the plastic bag and make it into a little rabbit by tying the handles in a simple knot (see Figure 6). When it hops around on the floor and sniffs and nibbles, students are usually quite amazed.

Ask the students, "What exactly is a puppet? Can someone give me a definition?"

Gather responses on the board and find common ideas. When I do this I like to offer examples that both support and challenge

Figure 6 Bunny bag.

student definitions. Most of the time students will say things like "A doll that you make that you move." Use the "eyeball" puppet to demonstrate that a puppet is not necessarily an object that is separate from a human manipulator—in this example, the human body *is* part of the puppet! If you don't have the "eyeballs" just draw some eyes on your knuckles with a washable marker and make your hand talk! The picture included of a mask interacting with a human hand (it played a soul character in Homer's Odyssey) also challenges traditional expectations (see Figure 7).

Compare the students' answers with some famous definitions of a puppet. Here are a few. Do you think they are accurate?

Bill Baird: "A puppet is an inanimate object that is made to move by human effort in front of an audience."

My problem with this definition is that it ignores puppets that are not used for performance. A child playing with a puppet by themselves is still using a puppet!

Roger Daniel Bensky (translated by Henryk Jurkowski): "The puppet is, in exact terms, a mobile object, un-derived, made for dramatic action, operated either visibly or invisibly by

Figure 7 A soul puppet.

whatever techniques its inventor has chosen. Its use is for theatrical performance."

This one is fun to take apart with students. They like to figure out what exactly some of these terms mean, like "un-derived."

Cheryl Henson: "A puppet is an object that appears to be alive when manipulated by a human hand."

I like the simplicity of this one! It's also fun to share because you can debate what counts as an "object."

Planning

Put students in groups of three. Each group needs three trash bags and a space to work at a table that is big enough for all group members to stand next to each other on the same side of the table.

Some rules: Puppeteers are *not* allowed to talk while performing with this puppet. Plastic bags may not be tightly tied together or permanently modified in any way.

Task 1: Assemble a human puppet using only plastic bags

Usually I have two volunteers demonstrate with me first so everyone understands what to do.

Puppeteer 1 will operate the head and right arm.

Puppeteer 2 will operate the left arm and waist.

Puppeteer 3 will operate the feet.

Puppeteers are arranged based on the Japanese puppetry tradition of Bun Raku (for more about Bun Raku see p. 143). See Figure 8 for where puppeteers should stand.

Assemble the bags like Figures 9, 10, and 11.

Figure 8 Bun Raku puppeteering.

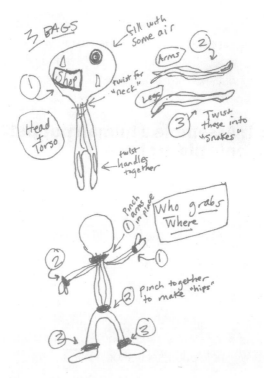

Figure 9 Plastic bag instructions.

Figure 10 Plastic bag puppet 1.

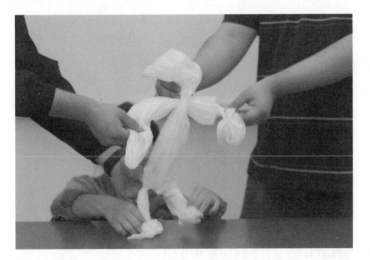

Figure 11 Plastic bag puppet 2.

After demonstrating how to put the puppet together, allow some time for groups to experiment with making the puppet walk. Remind them that when they perform they can't talk to each other or cue one another verbally. Ask them what helps them know what to do and what makes it more difficult.

At this point I coach them to make the puppet inhale and exhale, and explain that breathing is essential to creating a believable puppet. Switch roles until everyone has tried all three puppeteer positions and experienced breathing and walking from each position. Students should decide who will perform each part based on what the group feels was the most effective arrangement (or the teacher can assign the roles).

Task 2: Movement challenge!

Each group will perform their puppet on a tabletop "stage." The puppet must walk into a "meadow," sit down, breathe, perform a gesture that it does all the time, get back up, and exit for a specific reason. For advanced students, add the additional requirement that the puppet must break at least one law of physics. The audience needs to be able to identify the gesture, describe what mood the puppet is in, and explain why it leaves.

Suggestions if the students need prompting:

Common gestures: sneezing, scratching, fixing their appearance, waving, picking a flower, swatting a fly, nodding off for a nap, etc.

Reasons to exit: realizing they are late, seeing a friend, running away from something scary, being blown away by wind, etc.

Allow time for rehearsal (depending on the age of the group— middle school students and above need at least fifteen minutes).

Sharing effective work

Have each group present their puppetry. After each group performs, ask the following questions to the audience:

1 What gestures did you see? Were they clear?
2 What mood was the puppet in? Could you tell?
3 Why did the puppet leave?

After the audience responds, ask the performers to share what they were communicating. Ask all of the students to identify the moments where the puppet movement was the most "believable." Invite everyone to suggest "what ifs" that might make the manipulation more clear or believable.

Examples for good "what ifs":

1 What if the puppet breathed just like you would in that situation?

2 What if the puppet reacted more strongly to the environment around it?

3 What if you showed the audience the moment the puppet decides to leave? How could you do that?

Allow time for the students to integrate the feedback into a repeat performance. This "culminating" performance can be assessed using the "Collaborative Puppetry Rubric."

Task 3: Emotion Olympics

Reassemble your puppets. Now you need to respond as the puppet (no talking!) to create the following emotions.

- Anger
- Fear
- Joy
- Boredom
- Love

Note: The teacher should call out each emotion and observe how all the puppets respond. The teacher can have specific groups replay to share effective work. Encourage students to exaggerate the movement in the way that only puppets can, for example, can the puppet become so angry it literally explodes? Or so in love it literally floats up into the air?

Task 4: Not only human

Based on how the groups are functioning, you can leave them in groups of three for this next task or rearrange the groups into new groups of four, this will ensure the students have a chance to collaborate with different people.

Tell the students that for the next puppet challenge, each group will have more bags to work with and possibly more puppeteers. They must collaborate to create their own nonhuman creature and make sure it's really different from humans.

Rules:

1 Every group member must manipulate the puppet at once.

2 The puppet must do the same sequence that the human puppet did but according to its anatomy. Does it have four legs? No legs? How does it move? It can be any creature they come up with, as long as the movement is clear!

Share just as before, but start with these questions to the audience:

What kind of creature did you see? How was it different from a human?

Reflections, connections, and next directions

Lead a discussion or do a reflective writing assignment based on these questions.

1 What is a puppet? Has your definition changed?

2 What makes good puppetry?

3 What skills does a good puppeteer need to have?

4 What can puppets do that human actors can't?

Assessment checklist

Look for the following in student performances. Note whether each group accomplishes the following, or document their level of skill. (I use a 1-2-3 system, with 1 being "excellent," 2 "sufficient," and 3 being "not quite there yet.")

1 All students collaborate to manipulate one puppet.

2 The puppet has a character and all puppeteers support it.

3 The movement of the puppet makes sense · according to its "anatomy" or structure.

4 The puppet performs at least one clear gesture that supports its mood.

5 The puppet has a clear motivation for leaving a scene.

6 The group improves their puppet's performance after listening to group feedback.

---

4 Head, Hands, and Heart

Suggested age range

Seven to adult.

Time needed

60–90 minutes.

The big question

How do puppeteers create believable puppet movement?

Materials/preparation

Paper mask templates photocopied onto cardstock, one
per student plus a few extra.
Premade masks for the teacher to demonstrate with (see
Figure 12 for materials).
Scissors.
Staplers and staples.
Masking or scotch tape.
Fabric squares or old scarves at least 2 feet long on each
side, one per student. They need to drape well (lighter
fabrics work best). They will be taped or stapled but not
otherwise harmed.
Large rubber bands, two to three per student.

Boundaries and safety

Puppets should not talk for these exercises so that students really focus on movement. Sometimes I allow expressive sounds, but not words.

Assessment strategies

These activities allow for an opportunity for students to replay scenes after hearing feedback from their peers and the teacher. This allows for direct observation of improvement in their work. Can they listen to ideas and then incorporate them into improved work? Watch their performances carefully and be prepared to be delighted.

Figure 12 Materials for the "Mask" hand puppet.

Opening/hook

Let students know their hands and arms are about to get a workout so they need to warm up their hands. Here are some of my favorite hand warmups:

Hand shake: Students should shake their hands firmly and quickly for at least forty-five seconds. Freeze them. See who can feel their hands tingle. Why do they think that happens?

Finger waves: Students should hold their arms straight in front, palms up. Have them roll their fingers closed, pinky to thumb, like a wave, then roll them open again the opposite way (thumb to pinky). They should repeat this several times. Encourage gentle stretching.

Wrist rolls: Students roll their wrists slowly. Coach them to switch directions so they get a good stretch.

Feel free to try any child-safe arm stretches. Encourage students to take breaks and stretch if they need to, as puppetry can be strenuous.

Show students the premade mask. Ask, "Who thinks this is a puppet?" Get some answers. Next move the mask slowly and make it "look" around at each student. Ask, "Is it a puppet yet?" Add one of your own hands and manipulate it as if it's the mask's hand (Figure 13). See if they think it's a puppet yet. Let them know there are many more puppets they will be able to make using just paper and fabric. They are going to explore how puppeteers manipulate puppets so that their movement is believable.

Planning

Have students help you pass out the mask templates, scissors, and tape.

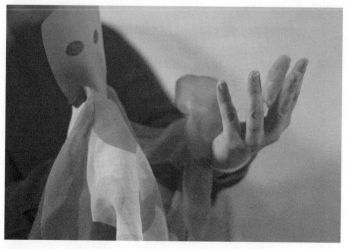

Figure 13 The puppeteer's hand becomes the puppet's hand.

Task 1: Head!

Construct your "mask head" from your template. Cut out the mask along its outline. Curve the paper gently to give it some dimension. Cut out the finger strip. This strip should go on the back of the mask so it can hold the mask against two of your fingers (middle and pointer fingers). Place it towards the bottom and give it a bit of a curve so you can fit your fingers behind it (see Figure 14). Tape or staple the strip in place. When

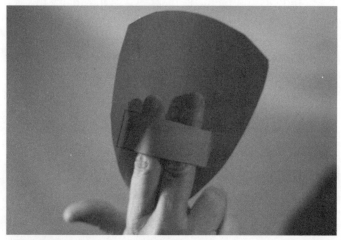

Figure 14 Back of the finger puppet.

Figure 15 Two paper head puppets.

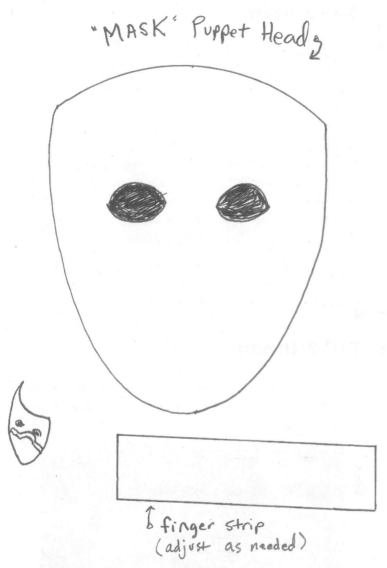

Figure 16 Pattern for a puppet mask.

your mask head is complete, put it on your dominant hand and practice moving the puppet until the rest of the group are finished. These puppets are meant to be performed on a tabletop (Figures 15 and 16).

Task 2: Heart!

Find a partner to work on eye focus. There are eyes drawn on the mask because in puppetry it is essential to make any puppet look like its eyes are perfectly focused on whatever it's looking at (Figure 17). Eye focus is the "heart" of a puppet—it makes the audience believe the puppet is experiencing emotions. With your partner, discover the focus of your puppet. When does it look like it's directly looking at your partner? Have your partner slowly move their hand and make your puppet follow it with its eyes. Your partner should let you know when the puppet loses its focus. Make sure to take turns until you both feel confident that you can make your puppet focus where you want.

Note: If students are young, they may benefit from putting a 3-dimensional nose on their puppet, like gluing on a pom pom, so they have more reference for the puppet's focus.

Task 3: Hands!

Students will need one scarf/fabric square, a stapler or tape, and one rubber band. Attach your fabric behind the chin of your

Figure 17 Eye focus is the "heart" of a puppet.

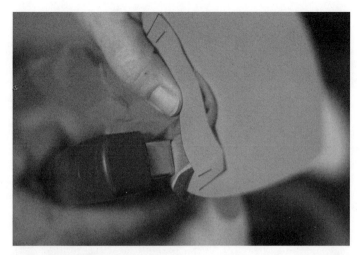

Figure 18 Stapling a scarf to card.

mask using staples or tape. Put the mask on your dominant hand. Use the rubber band to attach a corner of your fabric to your wrist (see Figure 13). You may need your partner to help you. It should look like the fabric is the puppet's body and your hand is the puppet's hand.

Optional—if you have some inexpensive gloves available, you can simply staple or attach one glove to a corner of the scarf. This may be easier for some children than the rubber bands.

Task 4: Put them together!

With your partner's help, practice creating the puppet's movement while keeping it focused correctly. How can you make your own hand look like it belongs to the puppet? Move slowly and try exaggerating the movement. Practice making your puppet do one clear movement at a time. Can you and your partner help each other perform the following actions:

- Breathe
- Wait for a bus

Figure 19 A scarf being moved.

- Look for a lost pencil
- Sneeze and recover
- Try not to fall asleep
- Call an imaginary pet to you

Task 5: Scenes with a partner

Tell students: Now you will work together to create scenes between your two puppet characters. Both students should stand behind the same side of the table. Try the following:

1 Have your puppets meet each other for the first time. How many different ways can your puppets greet each other? How can you create a puppet's personality through its handshake? How can you show that your puppets have really different personalities?

2 Have your puppets discover an object together (you can use anything handy like a pencil or sunglasses). They have never seen the object before. Let them figure out what the object does.

3 Have one puppet start the scene overwhelmed with sadness. Have the second puppet enter, notice the sad one, and try to cheer them up. By the end of the scene, both puppets should feel the same emotion. Improvise how that might happen.

4 Have your puppets go watch a scary movie together. Make sure it looks like they are watching the same thing at the same time.

Tell students to pick their favorite scene and practice it before sharing it with the rest of the group. If you have time, share more than one!

Sharing effective work

After each pair of students shares their performance, ask the audience if the movement was clear. Did they understand what was happening? Ask them to point out specific moments when the puppetry was most believable. Allow the performers to replay their work and watch carefully for improvement.

Reflections, connections, and next directions

Discussion prompts: How do you feel when you watch a really effective puppeteer? What kind of things kept you interested in the scenes? When you were puppeteering, what did it feel like when you were performing believable movement? Where was your focus? Were you thinking as if you were the character?

It's fun to talk about how puppetry requires a different sort of concentration than other forms of performance. Some students will feel like they are embodying the puppet, others might mention how the puppet "knew what it wanted to do" and they just helped it along. Many puppeteers experience that and describe it as almost like a trance. Psychologist Mihaly Csikszentmihalyi calls this highly concentrated state "flow" and has determined that it is the optimum state for learning.

It's also very useful to show students examples of professional puppeteers in performance (or better yet, invite a professional puppet company to perform) and discuss what makes the puppetry effective.

5 Everyday Object Puppets

Suggested age range

Five and upwards.

Time needed

60–90 minutes.

The big questions

How can we create characters from objects? How does the voice help create a character?

Materials/preparation

Bring in a variety of safe, clean, unbreakable household items for these exercises. It is best to find one object per student. They can also bring in something from home. I have a selection of objects commonly found in recycling bins or at thrift stores, discount grocery stores, and garage sales that I keep for workshops, including:

A variety of sponges
A variety of cleaning brushes
Cartons
Tongs
Whisks

Measuring cups and spoons
Colanders and strainers
Can openers
Garlic presses
Pitchers
Salt and pepper shakers
Rubber gloves
Plastic utensils, serving spoons, etc.

Any unusual gadgets that inspire you. I have a lot of interesting citrus squeezers that go over well.

Boundaries and Safety

Any time students do vocal exercises, they need to understand they are not to strain their voices. Their volume must be low. They must avoid using scratchy or gravely voices at this stage because if it is not done properly it can damage their vocal chords.

Assessment strategies

Listen to vocal choices for evidence of student mastery of techniques. See Figure 20 for an optional worksheet for students to document their choices.

Opening/hook

Choose your favorite object to use as a demonstration or group exploration. Ask the students to sit in a circle on the floor with you. Sometimes I put my box of objects in the middle to catch their interest if I trust they will be able to wait before touching them.

Show students your chosen object. Let's say it is a whisk.

Ask: If this object could talk, what would its voice sound like? What would it be interested in? What would it be worried about? How can we use the qualities of this object to create a voice? Let's come up with a voice for this whisk.

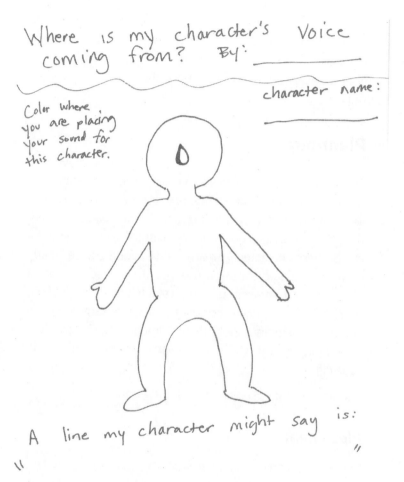

Where is my character's Voice coming from? By: _____

character name:

_____

Color where you are placing your sound for this character.

A line my character might say is:

"

"

Figure 20 Voice worksheet.

Encourage the group to brainstorm adjectives that describe the object. Some examples for a whisk would be: wiry, airy, open, stiff, shiny, springy. Often I write these on a big piece of paper.

Pick an adjective to start with. Let's say you choose "airy." Ask students what a voice would sound like if there were lots of air in a person's head. Go around the circle and have each child use an airy voice to say the line "Hello, I'm a whisk. Nice to meet you," whilst they move the whisk as if it were a puppet.

Planning

Students will need to know some basic vocal techniques in order to be successful with the next task. Inevitably, students will bring up the talking teapot and spoon characters from the Disney movie *Beauty and the Beast*. If you like, show a clip of these characters and analyze the vocal choices made by the voice actors. I often use popular characters from a variety of media as examples. I can teach how to do all of the characters from *Sponge Bob Squarepants*, for example, which impresses them and hooks them immediately. The problem is keeping up with what is popular and what you can do yourself!

Have students stand up and try out these concepts with you.

Placement

Where can sound come from in your body? Ask students to take a deep breath in. Watch them as they do this. Are they lifting their shoulders up? If so, they need to try again and breathe so their stomach goes out. I put my hands flat on my stomach and demonstrate how my fingers move away from each other when I breathe properly. This allows more air to be available for vocal work.

Explore the places you can put your breath and voice to create characters.

Tummy

Take a deep breath that goes into your tummy. This is where a lot of deep character voices are placed. Have students try the line "I'm a giant and I'll grind your bones to make my bread." I usually say the line as a giant and have the group repeat it all together. Brainstorm characters that might have a tummy voice. Good ones are slow turtles, forgetful characters, and monsters.

Chest

Breathy and brassy voices come from the chest. For a brassy sound, put your breath and focus into your chest as you breathe, and try to sound like Ethel Merman (they won't know who she is, but they'll love it). Try the line "There's no business like show business." Brassy sounds are loud and sometimes jarring. Brainstorm characters that might have a brassy chest voice. Loud and obnoxious characters will often be mentioned. Pirate voices are fun to try from the chest.

Breathy voices also come from the chest. Try saying "Happy birthday, Mr. President" in your best Marilyn Monroe voice. Try "Yeah, dude, let's go surfing" in a beachy California voice. Brainstorm characters that might be breathy.

Nose

Nasal voices are a lot of fun because they can create a sound very different from your everyday voice. Concentrate on pushing air into your nose and try a witchy line: "I'll get you my pretty, and your little dog too!" Make sure to try a witchy laugh. Try a whiny character. A good line for that is "No, Mom, I don't want Harry to have my ice cream." Brainstorm characters that might have a nasal voice. Nerdy scientists, cats, and stuck up characters sound good with nasal voices.

Head

Encourage the group to yawn with you. Yawning puts your soft palate in a great position for creating a head voice. While using a "yawn" position, try a good fairy character and say "Come out, come out wherever you are, and meet the young lady who fell from a star." Mickey Mouse has a head voice. Brainstorm other characters who could have this kind of voice.

Combinations/other

Some voices come from several places. I often voice small animals such as mice and chipmunks using a combination of head and nose placement. You can also use a tightened throat to sound like Kermit the Frog or Marvin the Martian. Make sure you are not straining if you do. See if the students have any unusual combinations to share. Often they can do wonderful imitations of famous characters. See if they can figure out where they are placing their sound.

Other tools: Mouth shape

Often if you look at a character and think about what its teeth are like, you can literally put your mouth in that position to create a unique voice. I literally stick my teeth out to create rodent voices and open my mouth really wide when doing a shark (like there isn't enough room for all my teeth). Scooby Doo is a fun example. The talented voice actor behind this character imagined how a dog's mouth shape would effect its voice. Try his line, "Rokay, Shaggy, ret's go" with the students.

Other tools: Accents

Trying different accents can be really fun and a great tool for creating characters (I am partial to the Valley Girl accent from California). However, make sure the students are avoiding stereotypes. If you have access to examples of real people speaking with an accent for students to imitate, it tends to prevent stereotypical portrayals.

Task 1: Object into character voices

Let each student choose an object (or hand them out randomly if students will respond better). Hand out voice worksheets if you choose to use them.

Tell students: You will create a puppet character out of your object. Start by creating a voice for them. Think of three adjectives that describe your object and tell them to your partner. When you both have three, write them on your worksheets. Where could you place your voice to create these qualities in your character?

Improvise some things your character might say. Try out a few different voices until you discover one that feels right. Write down a line your character says that helps you do its voice (or have your partner help you remember a good one). Mark where your best character voice is placed on your worksheet.

Share voices by going around the group and having each object puppet say their line. Students should move the objects as if they are speaking. Can the audience tell where the voice is placed? Can they guess the adjectives the puppeteer used to create the voice?

Task 2: Introductions

Have each object puppet introduce themselves to another object puppet using their character voice. Improvise a conversation that causes them to laugh so you can figure out that aspect of your character. Ask: Is it easy or difficult to keep your character voice? How can you help get the voice to come back?

Often puppeteers will use a catchphrase or specific laugh to help them find their character voices if they find them hard to recreate. See if students can use those tools.

Task 3: The kitchen family

Put students in groups of four and have them use the floor or a tabletop for their stage.

Tell students: Your object puppets are now characters in a sitcom. They are all part of a wacky family. Improvise a scene showing each object's role in the family and how it gets along with the other objects. Objects may not touch each other and cannot get into fights. One character needs to have a problem that the other characters help solve. Here are some opening lines to try if you need inspiration:

"I can't find an outfit for the kitchen fashion show!"

"Mom/Dad says I can't help make a cake because I'm too young!"

"Sister/Brother is making fun of me because I really need to visit the dishwasher!"

Allow groups time to rehearse.

Sharing effective work

After each group performs, allow time for audience feedback. Ask the audience to point out successful vocal techniques that the performers used to create their character voices.

Reflections, connections, and next directions

I find it quite effective to move directly from improvisation into writing. Have students write out the dialogue from their scenes, or write a story about their object character. Once they have found a character voice, it's often easier to imagine and write what it would do and say.

6 The Power of Design

Puppet Metaphors

Introduction

One of the most fun things to watch students discover is how a puppet can embody abstraction. Instead of creating a character who sneezes a lot, for example, a puppet can be the very "essence" of a cold! It could be a sneeze that has literally come to life. How can students use the elements of art such as color, shape, texture, pattern, and form *and* abstract movement to design and create a metaphorical character? Believe it or not, most young children are incredibly good at thinking this way with little coaxing. We tend to become more literal and rigid thinkers as we get older. Older students may seek "permission" or approval to create a really unique and unrealistic character. One of the ways I help students "break through" their rigid thinking is to provide a strict time limit for the puppet making process. When students have only a limited time to make choices, they are forced to accept quick solutions instead of "overthink" their work. This process is important to foster a flow of ideas that are free from self judgment. As an improvisation teacher as well as puppeteer, I have found (thanks to Viola Spolin) that an environment free of approval-seeking behavior is crucial for fostering true creativity.

Students should have free choice of materials and construction methods for this lesson. This open format for puppet building has specific educational purposes and is called "free-form" puppet making. Tamra Hunt and Nancy Renfro first articulated the benefits of this approach in *Puppetry in Early Childhood Education* (1982), which is hard to find but a treasure. Free-form choice of materials allows students to explore, experiment, make do with what is available, and solve problems. If students are just copying something or following exact directions the process is not nearly as challenging or rich. Ironically, providing a clear lesson structure is a big part of successful free-form puppet-making lessons. Hopefully this example will help inspire you to apply this technique to other types of lessons.

Suggested age range

Five and up.

Time needed

60–90 minutes.

The big questions

How can I choose materials and use the elements of visual art to create a puppet character? How can a character be abstract? What is a realistic character?

Materials/preparation

Scrap fabric of a wide variety of colors, patterns, texture, and thicknesses (you do not need much of each type of fabric but you do need lots of choices for students. Parents and community partners can be a great source for fabrics. Consider getting a big bin for your classroom to collect fabric donations throughout the year).

Scissors that work well on fabric.

Staplers and staples (staple pliers are great if you can find some).

Child-friendly adhesives that are strong enough for fabric. "Tacky glue" is a type that works well, and I have had good results with double-sided tape. Hot glue guns are an option if students are old enough or there are enough adult helpers to directly supervise or do the gluing for children. Do *not* let young children use hot glue guns.

Chopsticks, coat hangers, paint stirrers, and other inexpensive things that can serve as rods and sticks

Recycled, clean materials such as paper towel rolls and egg cartons, unused picnic items such as paper plates, plastic containers, foam shapes, and anything else that would work to give shape/volume to a puppet design.

Yarn, tissue paper, construction paper, chenille stems/pipe cleaners, or anything to give secondary movement to a puppet design (usually this is hair or something that moves independently of the direct action of the puppeteer).

Pom poms, googly eyes, "fun foam" pieces, felt, and any other craft items you think are fun to touch and move. Tactile interaction is a powerful and engaging activity for most students.

Organizing these materials can be tricky. Often for younger children I will divide materials for use by table groups to control the chaos. "Stations" for puppet supplies work well so students have access to all of the options available. If you have help, aides can supervise each station and provide one-on-one help with construction.

It can be very helpful to create an example puppet to share with students.

Make sure to print out "Dwarf Word" cards to distribute to students (see p. 63).

Boundaries and safety

Puppets will need time to dry before they are used. Make sure students know that puppets should not touch each other. Make sure to explain/demonstrate how your chosen adhesives will be used.

Opening/hook

Optional: If you have time, ask students to name as many kinds of
puppets as they can and discuss their characteristics (see Chapter
5). Make examples of these puppet types yourself (I recommend
Sneezy and Snobby, see Figure 21) and share them.

Figure 21 "Sneezy" and "Snobby" puppets.

Figure 22 Realistic rabbit puppet.

Start by explaining the difference between a realistic puppet and an abstract puppet. A realistic puppet (like the rabbit hand puppet in Figure 22) is meant to look just like something from real life (or very close to it). An abstract puppet communicates an idea, feeling, or other abstraction and looks like it is from another world (like Sneezy and Snobby).

Task 1: 20-minute "Dwarf Word" puppet

Tell students that they are going to design their own puppet and they can make any type of puppet they like, but they will only have twenty minutes to build it. Their puppet must be based on a "7 dwarves word" and be an abstract representation of that word (a visual metaphor). That means the design choices they make are very important. What color is their word? What shape would this word be if it came to life? What kind of movements make you think of this word? Tell them to keep their word a secret because the group will try to guess everyone's word when the puppets are shared. Each puppeteer will need to share a short performance of their puppet (thirty seconds or so)—but they are not allowed to use words—just sounds.

Distribute the "Dwarf Words" and make sure they are kept secret. I usually have to have some extras ready in case students are not sure what a word means and want to trade for one they are more comfortable with. I reserve this option for students who are really struggling.

Start a 20-minute countdown. Be prepared to give "warnings" every five minutes.

Tips: I almost always give students a little more time if they need it, but pretend to be very strict at first. If students will not stop (which happens often), I reserve the right to collect scissors and glue. Puppets don't have to be completely perfect—just usable for the lesson.

Sharing effective work

Have each student present their puppet. Make sure students clearly perform some movement and sounds to help express their character. Have the audience guess the word that inspired each puppet (it's okay if it isn't obvious—it's the guessing that's fun). Have the audience describe the design elements they see in the puppet that help express the word. Invite the designer to describe their experience and choices. Did they have to adjust their choices due to the time limit? Here are some prompts you can use to guide discussion:

What colors did the designer choose? What do they make you think about?

Is a specific part of the puppet emphasized? Why do you think the designer did that?

Is the puppet designer's interpretation of this word different from your own? Did anything surprise you about their interpretation?

One of the intrinsic lessons in this time limited, free-form building process is the need to let go of perfectionism and move forward. Watch students as they struggle and then see how much their effort pays off in the end. It's extremely rewarding to see as an educator.

Task 2 (optional, depending on time available): Improvised scenes

Put students into pairs or groups of three with their puppets. Random pairings seem to work the best. Have each group work at a table or find a space in the room where they can sit together.

Tell students: You will use your puppets to improvise a scene that shows what would happen if these puppet characters met each other for the first time. You can use words now. Some students jump right in to scenes but some may need structure. Here's a possible structure for the scenes:

Puppet 1: enters and is overwhelmed by their "Dwarf Word" and says something they want.

Puppet 2: enters and watches Puppet 1, then responds to Puppet 1 in character.

Puppet 3 (optional): enters and responds to what is happening.

Puppets 2 (and 3): help(s) Puppet 1 get what they want.

For example, Sneezy puppet enters loudly sneezing and complaining. She says, "I wish I could stop sneezing!"

Snobby puppet enters and watches Sneezy. He says, "My word, how rude, would you please stop getting your germs everywhere!"

Happy puppet enters and says, "She can't help it! It's her allergies!"

Snobby and Happy puppets see a cat that has been causing the sneezing and make it go away.

Sneezy puppet is grateful and they all hug.

(Feel free to demonstrate this with your own example puppets.)

Figure 23 "Sneezy" puppet.

Figure 24 "Snobby" puppet.

Sharing effective work

After each group performs for the rest of the class, allow time for audience feedback. What are some things the designers did that added to the performance?

It's interesting to compare this activity with the Object Puppets activity in Chapter 5. How does it change how you look at puppetry when you are focusing primarily on the choices of a designer rather than the performance of a puppet character?

Reflections, connections, and next directions

The lessons learned from this activity are great preparation for interpreting characters from a story. For example, if you were going to make puppets for the Three Little Pigs, how could you use design to show the different personalities of each pig? Can you give each pig a word to help guide its character design?

7 DWARVES WORD CARDS

Happy	Dopey	Bashful
Grumpy	Sneezy	Sleepy
Clumsy	Lazy	Forgetful
Brainy	Greedy	Afraid
Gloomy	Angry	Snobby
Lovey	Crazy	Sporty
Joyful	Bossy	Silly
Sassy	Excited	Scary
Fancy	Chatty	Messy
Cool	Giggly	Fluffy

7 *Chakabesh Traps the Sun*

Shadow Puppets and Storytelling

Suggested age range

Nine to adult.

Time needed

Minimum one 90-minute session (if you eliminate the
storyboarding and trust the class to work quickly and
independently in small groups).

With storyboarding, it works well to do that in a
preliminary session of 45 minutes or so, followed by at
least one 60-minute session for puppet making.

The big questions

What can shadow puppets do with only two dimensions,
light, and shadow? How can we tell a story using
shadow puppets?

Materials/preparation

Something to project on, such as a flat, white, cotton
  bed sheet (it is best to find something the students
  can stand behind and see through when performing).
An overhead projector (yes, these are outdated but
  absolute gold for a puppeteer because they allow for
  multiple surfaces for the puppets to perform on. If you
  don't have one, hang your sheet in a sunny doorway or
  experiment with a digital projector).
Example shadow puppets for demonstration (Figures 25
  and 26).
Copies of *Chakabesh Traps the Sun* for each group.
Storyboard paper and pencils for each group.
Scissors (one pair per student).
Lots of thick paper you can cut with child-safe scissors. I use
  recycled cereal boxes, old office folders, recycled poster
  board, etc. It doesn't matter if anything is printed on the
  paper since you will only be able to see the shadows.
Masking tape or scotch tape, one roll per group.
Thin chopsticks or anything safe that can be used as rods,
  such as long straws, at least six per group.

Optional:
Brads and hole punchers to make moving parts.
Music to play behind the performance.

Boundaries and safety

Make sure students understand that rods must only be
  used to move the puppets. I tend to hold on to them
  and hand them out only when the students are ready to
  practice performing so I can keep an eye on things. In
  addition, paper puppets can be fragile. Puppets should
  not touch one another when manipulated.

Assessment strategies

A checklist for student performances is included.

Figure 25 Shadow puppet set up.

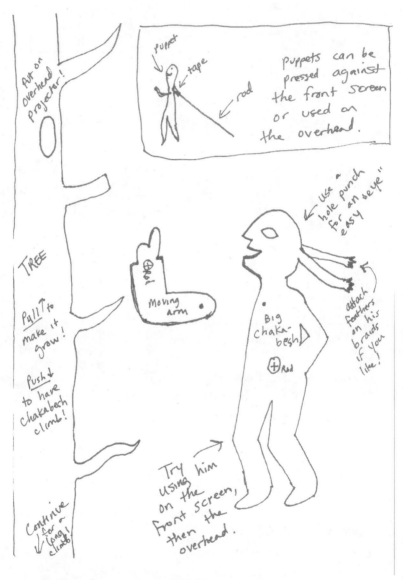

Figure 26 Shadow puppet templates.

Opening/hook

Set up the shadow puppet stage and demonstrate a shadow puppet. You can use the template provided to make Chakabesh, the main character, and the tree he climbs, or you can use your own creations. Model how a shadow puppet moves. Make sure to show how it grows and shrinks depending on how close it is to the screen or overhead. Show how it disappears if you turn it sideways quickly. Show how you can create the illusion of *perspective* using multiple puppets or by showing how the puppet changes when placed on the different screens.

Make sure to point out *positive* and *negative space*. A puppet that blocks the light (like the figure provided as an example) is using positive space. A puppet that lets the light shine through (like the outline of the figure left in the paper after it has been cut out) is using negative space. They will need to decide how to best tell the story using these tools.

Ask students: What kinds of illusions do you think you could create with a shadow puppet? Tell students they will interpret a Native American story from the Canadian Cree tribe using only light, shadow, and two dimensions. Show students the overhead projector or area they have to work within on the screen. They will need to know the size of the "stage" they have to work with.

Share the story *Chakabesh Traps the Sun*. Tell it as a storyteller would, or have students take turns reading out loud. This Cree story (provided) has been specifically adapted for this shadow puppet session. It is divided into five sections so that smaller groups of students can work on different parts. If you live near a Native American tribe or if you are teaching about a specific region, it is very easy to adapt any appropriate story that you find from recommended sources for your school district. The trick is to find something that lends itself to distinct playable parts for five to six groups.

Chakabesh Traps the Sun
A Cree story from Canada

1:

Once Chakabesh, the man as small as a boy but strong as a bear, looked up at the sky and said "I will go there today." His sister said, "No you will not!" but his mind was made up. He found the tallest tree and climbed to the very top. The sky was still far above him. Chakabesh had powerful medicine. He blew on the tree. This is the way he used his medicine to make it grow. It grew taller. He climbed to the top again, but it was not high enough to reach the sky. He blew on the tree and it grew taller and taller. But when he climbed to the top it was still not high enough. Finally, he used his medicine one more time. He blew on the tree until it was as tall as it would go. He climbed to the top and was surprised to see a road stretching across the sky.

2:

Chakabesh was very tired from all the climbing, so he lay down on the road to sleep. He was just starting to snore when a loud noise woke him up. He looked up and saw a light getting brighter and brighter and bigger and bigger. It was the sun! And Chakabesh was blocking its path.

"Get out of my way," said the sun. Chakabesh never did what anyone told him. He said "No. You go around me." The Sun replied, "I can't go around you, I must stay on my path or the world will catch fire. You wouldn't want that."

Chakabesh just laughed. "I will not get up for you or anyone. You'll have to jump over me if you want to get by." "Fine!" said the sun, and it stepped over Chakabesh. Sure enough, Chakabesh's clothes caught on fire as the sun went by. He had to use his most powerful medicine to stop the burning. The sun laughed at Chakabesh because he was burned and his hair was singed off.

3:

Chakabesh angrily ran home. His sister was waiting there for him. He told her, "The sun burned me. I was just sitting there minding my own business and he burned me. I am going to get revenge." His sister, who knew him well, said "Are you sure that's how it went? Don't do anything to the sun. You will just cause trouble for everyone." But Chakabesh didn't listen. He made a giant net that was big enough to hold the sun. He carried it up the tallest tree and set a trap on the sun's path. When the sun came that way, he was caught in the net, and darkness covered the whole world. Chakabesh was happy, but his sister said "Let the sun go! This will turn out badly for us all."

4:

His sister was right. The world was dark. No plants would grow and no hunters could see in the dark. The people were hungry and cold. Everyone was angry and they told Chakabesh, "Let the sun go! We need him!"

Chakabesh said, "I can't! If I get close enough to free him I will be burned to death." The people bothered him and bothered him.

Some animals were also hungry and came to Chakabesh to offer help. Chakabesh agreed to carry them up the tree. Maybe because they were small one of them could hide behind a rope and gnaw through it, and the sun would not burn them.

5:

The turtle tried first, but he was too big. "Ouch!" he said and turned back before he was burned.

The rabbit tried next, but he was too big too. "Ouch!" she said and turned back before she was burned.

Even the squirrel tried, but he was too big. "Ouch!" he said and turned back before he was burned.

Finally the mouse tried it. She was so little that she could hide her whole body behind the rope where the sun couldn't reach her. She gnawed through it and the sun escaped.

Chakabesh was grateful but forgot to say thank you.

And then life went on as usual.

Planning

Divide students into five groups. Assign each group a section of the story (as numbered) and give them a copy to refer to. Pass out storyboard paper and pencils.

Tasks

If you wish, you can share some or all of the following requirements for their shadow puppets. Post these so they can refer to them often. Can they do the following:

1 Include at least one change of perspective (for example, have a character go from far away to close up).

2 Use positive space to create at least one character or setting.

3 Use negative space to create at least one character, setting, or effect.

4 Include at least one puppet with moving parts.

5 Create clear transitions for the beginning and end of the scene.

Task 1: Storyboard

As a group, make a storyboard of all the moments you will need to create to tell your part of the story. You will have the overhead projector and the screen to work with so you will need to decide how best to use them. Everyone needs to make at least one puppet and everyone must perform a puppet.

If you have internet access, encourage students to research Cree people so they can be more accurate with their depictions of their characters. Sometimes you can use images from the internet as a guide for puppet making.

Task 2: Puppet making

Using your storyboards as a guide, decide who will make which puppets. Feel free to create background images to show where the characters are. Use the materials provided and feel free to try them out on the shadow screen as you go. (If possible tape out the size of the stage they have to work with for each group so they know the area they must fill with the puppets). Rods can be taped onto the back of the puppets with masking tape. Often I will create a "hinge" out of the tape so the rod can move a little.

Task 3: Rehearsal

Decide who will narrate your part of the story. You can also assign people to play the characters. Practice moving the puppets while narrating and speaking.

Sharing effective work

Use the rehearsal process to share amongst the groups. Allow each group to practice their section and experiment with where the puppets work best. The other groups can watch and offer "what ifs." Allow time for the groups to rebuild if any discoveries are made. Allow groups to be inspired by one another and find ways to connect each section of the story smoothly. If they don't discover this themselves, show them some ways to block the light sources to help with transitions between groups.

Task 4: Perform the whole story!

Check to see if students have met the challenges for the puppet making. If the students are excited and motivated, consider rehearsing a bit more and then presenting the performance for an audience. Invite parents or other classes from their grade level.

Reflections, connections, and next directions

Lead a discussion or do a reflective writing/drawing assignment based on the following questions:

If you were going to tell this story again, what other way could you use shadow puppets? For example, if you used mostly positive space, how could you use more negative space? Which part of the shadow puppet story do you think used the puppets most effectively? Why?

If you have time, research the history of shadow puppetry. Pretty much every country in Asia has their own unique form of this incredible puppetry, which allows for deep exploration of cultures and storytelling traditions. There is a treasure trove of beautiful examples out there.

8 Puppetizing Children's Literature

Introduction

Puppetry is important to explore as a fine art, but one of its most powerful uses is as a teaching methodology. Just like creative drama, creative puppetry can activate any material and engage all learning styles, ages, and abilities. One of the easiest ways to use puppets is to "puppetize" literature.

"Puppetizing" is a useful term coined by Tamra Hunt and Nancy Renfro in their wonderful book *Puppetry in Early Childhood Education*:

> *Puppetizing is closely supervised by one or more adults who apply creative dramatic techniques to direct children in the use of puppets for acting out stories, poems, songs and such. With puppetization there is neither audience or stage; the children merely perform informally for one another. (1982, 19)*

My lesson plan *Chakabash Traps the Sun* is technically a puppetizing plan using literature, but it is geared for older children who can work in groups. Here is one for younger children that includes strategies that are more developmentally appropriate. I'm hoping this will serve as an example to inspire your own lessons with your favorite stories.

The Gingerbread Kid

By Johanna Smith

Suggested age range

Grade K, ages four to seven years.

Time needed

One 60-minute session.

Goals

Students will use a paper pattern to construct a puppet.
Students will identify and re-create a sequence from a
    story.

Materials/preparation

Premade or store bought puppets that the teacher can
    use to serve as the little old man, little old woman, cat,
    dog, and fox. If available add a goat, sheep, cow, and/or
    horse (or whatever seems like it would be fun to use).
Photocopies of the Gingerbread Kid pattern (Figure 2.7)
    onto cardstock (one per student plus extra), you may
    choose to precut them depending on the cutting skills
    of the students.
Crayons, markers (available age-appropriate coloring tools).
Scissors.
Craft sticks for stick puppets, or, for action-packed puppets
    that can run, paper tubes that securely hold little
    fingers, such as coin wrappers (I use dime and penny
    sized wrappers cut in half). You can also make these
    out of construction paper. You will need two per
    student plus extra.
Masking or scotch (cello) tape.
Optional: Post or write the Gingerbread Kid's line where all
    the children can easily see it. It is "Run run, as quick as I
    did, or you won't catch me, I'm the Gingerbread Kid!"

Assessment strategies

One of my favorite things to assess with this kind of "story" lesson is comprehension. Can students re-tell the story on their own? What does that tell you about their understanding of it?

Figure 27 Gingerbread Kid pattern.

Opening/hook

In an ideal world it would be wonderful if you could bake gingerbread with the class so they could experience how delicious it smells and tastes. If that is not possible, bring in a sachet of spices used to make gingerbread for the students to pass around and smell. If that is not possible, ask students: is there a kind of food that you love so much that you would run after it and chase it? Tell students you will be sharing a story about a delicious cookie called the Gingerbread Kid and the day it ran away from everyone who wanted to eat it.

Planning

Tell the story of the Gingerbread Kid (Figure 28). Here's a simple version. If you're feeling bold, memorize it and tell it using premade or store-bought animal puppets as you go.

Figure 28 Gingerbread Kid finger puppet.

The Gingerbread Kid
Retold by Johanna Smith

Once upon a time there lived a little old woman and a little old man. They lived in a lovely little old house on a little old farm. One day the little old man, who was a very good baker, felt a bit hungry so he decided to bake some gingerbread. He mixed all the ingredients in a great big bowl and carefully rolled out the dough. The little old woman came in to help. She decided to make the dough into the shape of a child. She gave it raisins for eyes and a cinnamon candy for the nose. Then they put the dough in the oven to bake. When it was time, the little old man and the little old woman opened the oven door to see if the gingerbread was done. Woosh! Out of the oven ran a gingerbread kid! The dough had come to life. As it sprinted to the front door, it laughed and sang, "Run run, as quick as I did, or you won't catch me, I'm the Gingerbread Kid!"

The little old woman and the little old man ran as fast as they could after the Kid, but they couldn't catch it.

Right outside the front door, a little cat was snoozing in the sun. She heard the racket from the kitchen and woke up just as the Gingerbread Kid jumped over her to escape. "Meow!" she said, and tried to catch it with her paws, but she just barely missed. "Oh no no no! You can't eat me!" said the Gingerbread Kid, and it ran down the front lawn singing "Run run, as quick as I did, or you won't catch me, I'm the Gingerbread Kid!" The cat was very fast, but she soon fell behind.

The Gingerbread Kid ran and ran until it reached the front gate. Waiting at the gate was a little dog. That Gingerbread Kid sure smelled good, so the dog said "Woof!" and jumped up to catch it in his mouth. "Oh no no no! You can't eat me!" said the Gingerbread Kid, and it jumped over the dog and ran away and sang "Run run, as quick as I did, or you won't catch me, I'm the Gingerbread Kid!" The dog tried to keep up, but soon fell behind.

(At this point you could add as many farm animals as you like to the story—such as a goat, a sheep, a cow, a horse, etc.—just follow the same structure and try to keep the order straight! It helps to go in order of size).

The Gingerbread Kid ran far ahead of everyone chasing it. Soon it came to a wide river. The Gingerbread Kid had to stop or it would get wet and fall apart. A fox came out from behind a tree. "I can take you across the river," said the fox. "I'm a great swimmer. Just hop on my tail and you'll stay dry."

Just then, everyone who was chasing the Gingerbread Kid came around the corner and yelled "There you are!" So the Gingerbread Kid somewhat reluctantly jumped on the fox's tail and they swam into the river. When they were well away from the bank of the river, the fox said, "The water is deeper than I thought. Why don't you come up on my back? It will be safer."

So the Gingerbread Kid carefully walked onto the fox's back. When they were in the middle of the river, the current became swift and the water rose higher and higher. The fox said, "You know what would be the safest place for you? My nose. Come stand on my nose and you definitely won't get wet."

So the Gingerbread Kid jumped from the fox's back, hoping to land on its nose. But the fox loved gingerbread too, and caught the Gingerbread Kid in its mouth and ate it all up.

And that was the end of the Gingerbread Kid.

Tell students they will be making their own puppet Gingerbread Kid and we will all tell this story together. Let them know that you will be playing the role of all the characters who chase the Gingerbread Kid.

Task 1: Puppet making

Have the students color the Gingerbread Kid patterns however they like, then carefully cut them out with scissors. Attach sticks to them, if using, or attach paper tubes on the back of the puppet's legs using tape or staplers. Adults might have to assist with this, or you can do this over a break such as lunchtime.

Sharing effective work

If there is time, have each child share their Gingerbread Kid and show the rest of the class how they will make the puppet run and say "Run run, as quick as I did, or you won't catch me, I'm the Gingerbread Kid!"

Task 2: Puppetizing

Decide where the story will take place in the classroom. Designate areas to be the house/kitchen, front door, front yard, gate, and the river. Gather students around the "kitchen" with their puppets hidden behind their backs so that when it is time they can "jump" out of the oven. You might also choose to put groups of "Kids" in each major area to divide up the story. Make sure they know to move slowly and that puppets cannot touch each other.

Narrate the story using the puppet characters as you go to interact with and chase the Gingerbread Kids. Prompt them to say their repeating line using their Gingerbread Kid voices. When the fox comes, I find it highly entertaining to do several rounds of swimming and eating so that all the Gingerbread Kids get a turn.

Task 3: Replay/assessment

If you have time, ask if the students want to replay the story and do the roles of the other characters too. Assign students to be the old couple, cat, dog, and fox. See if they can recall the order of the story, get in the proper places for their characters, and retell it in the correct sequence.

9 Puppetizing Science

A Cross-Disciplinary Plan for Younger Children

Introduction

Puppetizing can also be used to explore any subject, not just language arts. In addition, puppetry can make informational text a lot more exciting for children (and, to be honest, for teachers too). One of my favorite things to do is use puppetry to help students explore the natural world. This science lesson exploring coral reef ecosystems has been specifically designed and tested for five year olds and younger. It includes some puppet play as the hook to engage students in the topic, but this can be easily adapted or removed.

Make a Coral Reef Fish

By Johanna Smith

Suggested age range

Grade K, age five and under.

Time needed

Two 45-minute sessions.

Session 1: Design your reef fish

The big questions

What is "anatomy" and what body parts do fish have? What kinds of fish live in coral reefs? How have coral reef fish adapted to their environment? How do they protect themselves? Can we make our own puppet fish that could defend themselves in a coral reef?

Materials/preparation

Premade or bought fish and shark puppets (coral reef species).

Premade backdrop or projected image of a coral reef habitat.

Precut fish templates (Figure 29) photocopied onto cardstock (one per student, plus extra).

Crayons, markers (available age-appropriate coloring tools).

Scissors.

Craft sticks (one per student, plus extra).

Masking or Scotch (Sello) tape.

Glue sticks (one per student).

Construction paper in a variety of colors or premade fin shapes.

A source of information about coral reef habitats. We primarily used the book *Fishy Facts* (1997) by Anne Miranda prepared as a PowerPoint presentation. I have included some information to share (Figure 30), but you may choose to supplement with good sources of information online.

Assessment strategies

Observe fish puppets to see if they reflect understanding of fish anatomy and defenses in their design and construction. Can students explain their choices using appropriate vocabulary?

Figure 29 Fish patterns.

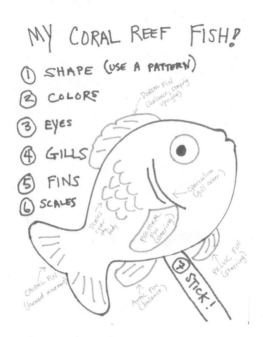

Figure 30 Fish puppet instructions.

Figure 31 Coral reef.

Opening/hook

Tell students you are especially excited about school today because you are going to take a field trip under the ocean. Introduce your companion the fish puppet.

Note: Manipulate the fish and shark puppets freely in front of you without trying to hide the fact that you're the one doing the voice (no ventriloquism necessary). Improvise dialogue or use suggested lines. You can also recruit help to be some of the characters.

> Fish: Hello children! I'm so excited to show you my home, the coral reef. I'm usually so lonely.
>
> Teacher: You look so sad. Why are you lonely?
>
> Fish: You see, there aren't any other fishes living in my reef right now.
>
> Teacher: Fish, I have a great idea.
>
> Fish: What?
>
> Teacher: My students can help you! They can make some fish to come live with you! Right, everyone?
>
> Fish: What a great idea! But there's a problem.
>
> Teacher: Uh oh.
>
> Fish: There's a shark living near my reef.
>
> Shark: (popping up quickly) Bwa ha ha! I'm hungry for fish!
>
> Fish: Go away, shark! You don't scare me! I know how to defend myself against you!
>
> Shark: We'll see about that. (swims away) Duh duhhh … Duh duhhh … (making fun of Jaws music)
>
> Fish: Okay, kids, I know you can trick that shark. I have to go check on my reef. See you there soon!
>
> Teacher: You all are going to design a fish that can live a long time on the reef, so it has to have a defense against being eaten. Luckily, coral reef fish have lots of defenses.

Planning

Present *Fishy Facts* by Anne Miranda or a similar source. Point out some parts of the coral reef: coral, seaweed, anemones, open water, rocks, etc.

Show examples of coral reef fish with the following defenses:

- Spots on their tails that act as a fake eye to trick predators into aiming for the wrong end of the fish.

- Camouflage to make the fish look like rocks or seaweed so predators can't find them.

- Bright colors to warn predators that the fish is poisonous or dangerous.

- Patterns like spots and stripes to confuse the predator, especially when fish swim together.

- Sharp teeth or spines to ward off predators.

- Use of poison in their own spines or borrowing poison protection from anenomes.

Share parts of a fish illustration, pointing out fins, scales, and operculum (gill cover). Point out that fish use gills to breathe oxygen from water so they need to make sure to put them on their fish.

Task 1: Puppet making

In table groups, hand out the fish patterns. Guide the students with the following instructions:

1 Draw your fishes *eyes*. Does it have a "fake" eye to trick the Shark?

2 Draw the *operculum* for your fish.

3 Draw a few *scales* so we remember they are there protecting your fish.

4 Color your fish making sure to choose *camouflage* or *bright colors*. Does your fish have a *pattern* that could confuse the shark or help it blend in with the seaweed?

5 Cut out *fins* for your fish (if you want point out the dorsal, pectoral, pelvic, caudal, and anal fin locations). Glue your fins in the right place.

6 Does your fish have *sharp* defenses like teeth or spines? Add them now using construction paper and glue.

7 Glue or tape your stick in place.

Sharing effective work

Have students show their fish and point out the defenses they included in their design.

Task 2: Puppetizing practice

Fish should reappear after the sharing process.

> *Fish: Wow, look at all my new fish friends! What wonderful defenses! Guess what everybody? There's one important defense we have if we work together, and that is swimming in a school. Let's try it!*

Divide students into small groups and help them arrange their puppets into a school. This can be done in many ways. We had students hold their fish puppets over their heads and move using their whole bodies. We picked one fish to be the leader and took turns "swimming" around the room.

The puppets can reappear to close the lesson.

> *Fish: Wow, I'm so excited to show you my reef. I'm not quite finished getting everything ready, so I'll be back tomorrow. I'm*

sure your defenses will beat that shark!
Shark: (pops up and laughs ominously) Bwa ha ha!

Session 2: Living on the reef

The big questions

Where is the best place for your fish to live on the coral
reef? What is a way fish can work together to defend
themselves?

Materials/preparation

Student-created fish puppets from session 1 (prepare
extra in case new students come in).
Fish and Shark puppets.
Backdrop showing the coral reef environment, including
open water, coral, seaweed, anemones, rocks, etc.

Assessment strategies

Observe to see if the students are able to successfully apply
their puppet fish defenses in the coral reef environment.
Have the students draw a fish or use a blank fish
template to show all the parts of a fish they remember.
See if they can remember all the defenses their fish could
use.

Opening/hook

Puppets should reappear.

Fish: I'm back everyone! It's time for our trip to my coral reef.
Shark: I am looking forward to eating ... I mean meeting ...

> all the new fish on the reef! I sure hope they don't have any
> defenses.
> Fish: Oh, they have defenses all right. You're not eating anyone
> today!
> Shark: We'll see. Bwa ha ha. (exits)
> Fish: Everyone, we need to practice swimming in a school one
> more time before we go. It's one of our best defenses.

Students should get their finished puppets and practice swimming with them.

Planning

Show students the coral reef backdrop (Figure 32) or projected image, pointing out the different places they could hide or use as defenses. Review defenses that coral reef fish might use against a hungry shark (review PowerPoint if needed).

Figure 32 Coral reef backdrop.

Task 1: Puppetizing

The shark character can be present and pop up occasionally to remind students that he is hungry and looking for fish without defenses. As students match their defenses with the proper location on the reef habitat, the shark should try to eat them and fail.

Using the backdrop or projected image as a performance area, call up each fish or small groups of fish to show how they use their defenses (Figure 33). Each defense should be in the following areas:

- Rocks and Seaweed: camouflage.
- Anemones: bright colors and patterns.
- Open water: false eyes, sharp poisonous spines, teeth, confusing patterns, bright colors.

As the shark attempts to "get" them and fails, he/she should become increasingly frustrated.

Figure 33 Fish puppets in front of the coral reef backdrop.

Have students join together in one big school and carefully swim around the classroom. The shark should get really confused and overwhelmed, showing how this strategy is a good defense.

The puppets can close the lesson.

> *Fish: Thank you so much everybody! I have so many new friends. We will live long happy lives on our coral reef thanks to these excellent defenses.*
> *Shark: Aw, phooey. I give up.*
> *Fish: See you at the reef!*

10 Puppet Filmmaking in the Classroom

Introduction

Puppet movies are a fantastic way to use all the technology that is now available in most public schools. Once you have access to a camera, it doesn't take many more resources to create entire worlds on film. Students of the current generation tend to think in images and are excellent editors. Those of us who grew up with less technology can step back and learn from them! In that spirit, I've included the major concepts to cover with the assumption that further research and training on current technology will be necessary for most teachers. However, if I can do this in the classroom, anyone can. Although, I would never have been able to do this without learning from puppet filmmaker Tim Lagasse who is an amazing teacher as well as artist.

Suggested age range

Nine to adult.

Time needed

Minimum three sessions of at least sixty minutes.

The big question

How do puppets work when the "stage" is a camera?

Materials/preparation

Cameras with simple movie software (iPads work very well).

Access to media storage. Most schools can provide access to a cloud storage service such as Dropbox so students can share large files. Check with the technical staff at your school in advance. Thumb drives (small portable storage devices) can be helpful too.

Old magazines with lots of landscape pictures. National Geographic is great. The students can draw landscapes themselves if you can't find magazines, but it's fun to use the pictures.

Scissors.

Construction paper.

Tape (clear tape is good).

Glue sticks and craft glue.

Paper templates or taped areas for students to work in that have a 4:3 aspect ratio, one per filmmaking group. That just means it is a rectangle four units by three units that matches the frame of an iPad camera. You will need to use another ratio if you are not using an iPad—always check first. It is easy to eyeball it if you have someone to assist you. Figure 34 is an example that you can easily enlarge.

Chopsticks or straws (whatever is safe and handy) to use as
  puppet rods.
Socks, buttons, scrap fabric, yarn, and other fun materials
  for more in-depth puppet making (if desired).
Demonstration image of a landscape that has a clear
  foreground, middleground, and background and
  premade example puppets. Use my image of the desert,
  pyramids, and camel puppet if you like—photocopy
  the puppet patterns and backgrounds included
  onto cardstock and cut them out (Figures 35 and 36).
  Use rods to move the puppets (you can use clear tape
  to attach them). Color them however you like.
Music to play for demonstration. The *Benny Hill* theme
  song (*Yakety Sax*) is good for this.
Nice to have:
Tripods.
Portable light source.
Microphones that are good enough to capture specific
  sounds and use for voice-overs.
Instruments to make sound effects.
Storyboard paper (there are free templates available online!).

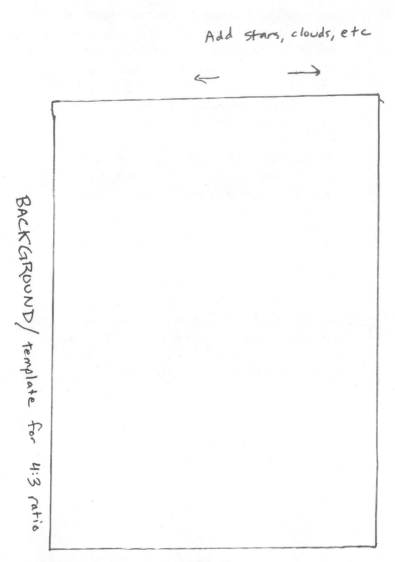

Add stars, clouds, etc

BACKGROUND/ template for 4:3 ratio

Figure 34 Background template, 4:3 aspect ratio.

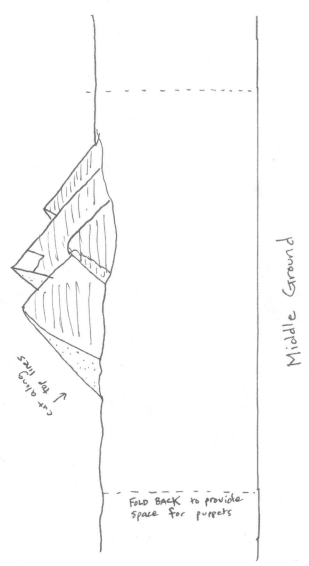

Middle Ground

Cut along dot lines

FOLD BACK to provide space for puppets

Figure 35 Middleground.

3 PUPPETS = 1 CHARACTER

③ Background

① FOREGROUND

② middle ground

Photocopy onto cardstock. Color + cut out the camels. Attach rods to manipulate. Use with Background + middle ground.

Figure 36 Camel puppets.

Opening/hook

Set up a camera so that it is focused on your example landscape. It is very convenient to put the image flat on a table top and use a tripod to point the camera straight down at it. If you can, connect the camera to a projector so the students can watch what you are doing live in real time. Show students how to frame the landscape (zoom in, focus, etc. so that the image in the camera shows the "stage" you want).

Play your music. While it is playing, make your background puppet run across the horizon until it is out of the frame. Switch puppets and have your middleground puppet run the other direction across the hills. Finally, bring in your foreground puppet and move them as if they are out of breath. They can run back to far away again if you are inspired.

Ask students to explain how you made it look like the puppet was one character moving toward the audience. Explain that puppets can be used to play tricks with perspective if you understand the concepts of foreground, middleground, and background. Point these out on your image and show how each example puppet is sized. In other words, hold up the puppets off camera and reveal the trick.

Tell students they will make their own short puppet film in their own landscape that creates the illusion of one puppet character moving from far away to up close (or close to far away).

Planning

Divide students into groups of three or so. Give each group a template or taped area to work in, a couple of magazines, scissors, glue sticks, and lots of construction paper.

Task

Task 1: Make a landscape

Let students know the area they have to work in represents the frame of the camera. If a puppet goes beyond the boundaries, they won't be seen.

Each team needs to create a two-dimensional landscape that includes a foreground, middleground, and background. These layers should remain separate (not glued together) so that puppets can be operated behind each layer. Use construction paper to make each layer. You can use the magazines to find ideas for landscapes. If you find an image that is large enough you may cut it out and use it in your landscape.

Figure 37 Hard at work.

Allow students an opportunity to check their landscapes through a camera to make sure the framing is working how they want.

Task 2: Make three versions of a puppet character

Students can create either two- or three-dimensional puppet characters for their movies, or a combination. Whatever creates an effective perspective illusion is fine. The puppets should be operated using rods, and puppeteers should make sure they are not in view during filming.

Tell students: Your job is to make at least three copies of a single puppet character that can move in the stage. The puppet character should appear close, far away, and somewhere in the middle, and show a variety of movements (running, walking, hopping, skipping, flying, etc.). You will film your character in one take.

Task 3: Filming

Make sure to have students practice using the camera pointing down at their landscape. Do not allow them to use preprogrammed editing tools. They need to shoot everything in one take. Their character can't speak but they can use music (without lyrics) and sound effects if they play them live. They can do as many takes as they need.

Task 4 (optional): Editing

Feel free to help students add music and sound postproduction.

Figure 38 Students prompted to create stories with their puppets and sets.

Figure 39 Figuring out how to get the best angle for a film.

Sharing effective work

Depending on your setup, you can have students play their movies directly from their cameras to the projector. The audience should point out successful work to the filmmakers after each one is shared. Sometimes I like to have students save their work as one digital file and share it with me. I edit them all together, add transitions and credits, and show them as a group.

Task 5: Movie making

Students can now add more characters to their landscape and film a short story. You can unify the films a bit by giving students a format to work with such as news reports or music videos. This process is usually really open-ended for me but it is important to cover a few things before letting them film.

Have them research the different kinds of camera shots they can use (often they will know these instinctively). When is a close-up

Figure 40 Children with finger puppets.

Figure 41 Fireman and truck puppet.

effective? What is a tracking shot? What are panning, tilting, and zooming? How can these techniques be used to most clearly tell their story?

Explore editing tools before storyboarding so they can plan transitions between shots. Make sure they know they can create transitions with the puppets and the camera too, not just the editing software. I like to keep firm limits on the transitions allowed (for example, allow only cuts and fades). This helps students focus on the storytelling and not how many cool effects they can put in their films.

When they have a good sense of these tools they should storyboard their movie and plan which shots they will do in what order before filming. If they do multiple shots, they need to keep track of the ones they plan to use. Sometimes I let them discover this the hard way.

Supervise the editing process to make sure all group members participate. Make sure they create a title and credits for their films.

Make sure they save their films as one digital file so you can collect them and edit them together. You don't have to do this but it looks really nice and makes it easier to share. I prepare DVDs of the film to give to each student.

Invite an audience of fellow students and parents and have a puppet movie night!

Reflections, connections, and next directions

Once students get the hang of using puppets as the subjects of films, inspire them to make more! Let them work on their own if they want to, or encourage them to take on specific filmmaking roles such as director, writer, puppet designer, camera operator, editor, and puppeteer.

Try these prompts to get them started:

- Tell a story from an object's point of view. What does a blade of grass experience every day? How can you show that?

- Put puppets in an everyday setting. What happens when human actors interact with them?

- How can you use a puppet to tell an animal's story? Use a realistic puppet and film outside.

- Create new creatures in new worlds. Can you tell a story that takes place on another planet?

11 Giant Puppets and Community Celebrations

Introduction

In 2016, I had the pleasure of designing and constructing a giant puppet with the students in room 17 at Sycamore Elementary School in Claremont, California, with host teacher Talia Bowman. We designed a puppet character that symbolized the spirit of Sycamore. Our character was written into a musical pageant to celebrate the 125th anniversary of the school. Other classrooms had roles in the pageant that were integrated into the performance. This lesson is different in that it's an account of what one group did, with the assumption you will adapt the process for your own needs.

Suggested age range

The puppet was done with nine to twelve year olds (combined 4th, 5th, and 6th grade classroom).

Time needed

For this project I visited the class for an introduction to giant puppets (about thirty minutes) followed by regular visits of ninety minutes once a week for about two months. I worked with groups of children in "rounds" of about twenty minutes each to make the paper maché process more manageable.

The big questions

How can we communicate the spirit of our school with a giant puppet? How can we use a giant puppet to celebrate our school and community?

Materials/preparation

For planning the task: Paper, pencils, slideshow of images of giant puppets from companies such as Bread and Puppet, the Puppeteer's Cooperative, and In the Heart of the Beast Theatre. An example giant puppet if you have one available.

For the puppet making (start gathering materials using parent/community help as early as possible):

Two to three flat cardboard sheets as large as you can find (large appliance boxes are good, but make sure there is just one layer of cardboard to cut).

Two to three plain, flat, cotton sheets (I dyed ours to match the puppet's color scheme).

Bamboo poles, at least 8 feet long and 2 inches in diameter for the majority of the length. If you cut bamboo, allow some time for it to dry before using it.

Markers.

Masking tape.

Duct tape.

Newspaper.

Your favorite paper mache materials. See detailed instructions included.

Utility knife for the teacher.

Scissors.

Twine.

Screwdriver or awl to poke holes with.

Water-based paint, brushes, clean up supplies, smocks.

Helpful: Staple pliers, cordless drill, sewing machine and necessary accessories.

Assessment strategies

Students provided proposals of their preferred designs which included drawings and written justifications. This evidence was very useful to determine how deeply they were thinking about their school and what would best represent its "spirit." The best evidence that students succeeded at this project was the successful construction and performance of the giant puppet.

Opening/hook

My favorite way to motivate a class for making giant puppets is to bring in and set up a giant puppet for them to try. However, with safety concerns in most schools, this is not always possible. Instead, ask students if they have ever seen a giant puppet and show them some images. Do a quick internet search for the Bread and Puppet Theatre and you will find a plethora of amazing giant puppets to show the class.

Share an example of a giant puppet and video of a puppet pageant celebrating a place and/or person (Bread and Puppet has done some incredible work on figures such as Chico Mendez if you need a place to start). Ask the students how we could do something similar for their school. What do they know about their school's history? What's important for people to know about it?

Real world result: In my case we brainstormed together briefly and narrowed the points down to some key ideas. Then I asked, "What image do you think would be the best thing to represent everything that Sycamore Elementary School means to you?" I helped them clarify their thoughts by drawing a few of their ideas for them. After a while it emerged that the group all agreed that the best representation of their school would be some sort of sentient sycamore tree.

Task 1: Design

Tell students: Draw a possible design for our puppet. Include written explanations to make sure we understand your ideas even if drawing isn't your strength. I will collect these and try to see which ideas are most frequently used and present my findings to you.

After looking through their work (for example, see Figures 42 and 43), I made a list of things that appeared that were

Figure 42 Caidan's design.

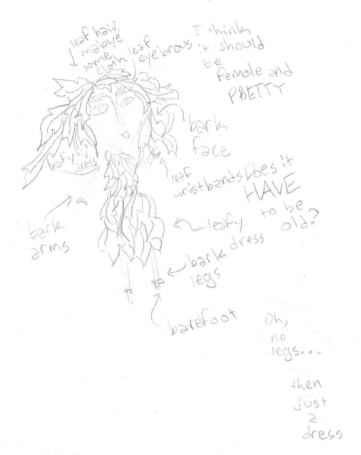

Figure 43 Frida's design.

strong concepts. I came back the next day for a quick visit and shared these results. Based on a list of dominant themes, we negotiated a design together out of the parts they liked the most from student designs. They decided on a two-headed sycamore tree spirit (Figure 44). I did my best to draw the final idea on the board. After this we felt ready to start construction.

Figure 44 Group design.

 Task 2: Teacher prep of head and hands

Using student designs as a reference, I used a mat knife to cut two identical hand shapes per hand out of cardboard. I stapled them together around the outside, leaving the bottom open like a "sleeve" so that we could later insert bamboo poles to manipulate them (Figure 45).

I also prepared the cardboard base of the puppet heads. See Figure 46 for how I did that, but also please download a copy of "How to Make Giant Puppets" by the Puppeteer's Cooperative in Boston. This resource is absolutely wonderful and offered for free on the web. You can find this information

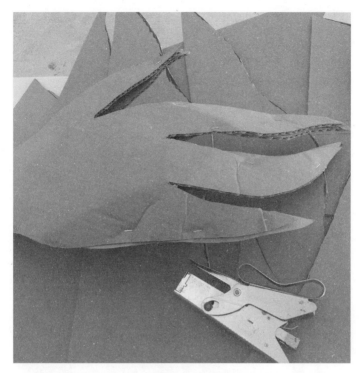

Figure 45 Using a stapler to create the hand.

as well as video tutorials and lots of other stuff on their website, https://puppetco-op.org. I learned a great deal of what I know from them.

Task 3: Newspaper sculpting and paper maché

Students worked with me in small groups to cover the cardboard heads with newspaper to give us a smooth surface to paper maché. They shaped eyebrows, noses, and lips out of newspaper and masking tape and attached them to the head. Then we paper machéd the whole thing over the course of several sessions (see detailed instructions for paper maché).

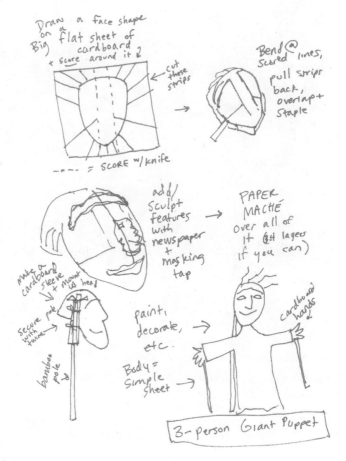

Draw a face shape on a Big flat sheet of cardboard + score around it

Bend @ scored lines, pull strips back, overlap + staple

← cut these strips

---- = SCORE w/knife

add/ sculpt features with newspaper + masking tap

PAPER MACHÉ over all of it (4 layers if you can)

make a cardboard sleeve + mount is head

Secure pole with twine

bamboo pole

paint, decorate, etc.

Body = simple sheet

cardboard hands

3- person Giant Puppet

Figure 46 Giant puppet how-to.

Task 4: Painting and decorating

Students helped me put a white base coat on the puppet heads and hands, and then paint them based on their designs (Figure 47). They collected scrap paper, traced sycamore tree leaves, and cut out multiple copies. We attached these all over the puppets and used them to make a beard on our male head. I brought in raffia to create hair for the girl head.

Figure 47 Painting the giant puppets.

Task 5: Teacher prep of head holders

I constructed a long cardboard box in each head. These held the bamboo head poles tightly. I drilled holes through the holder and pole and tied them together with twine so that the heads were firmly secured.

Figure 48 Students of Sycamore Elementary creating a giant puppet for a puppet pageant.

 # Task 6: Get dressed

Students brought in several old, flat sheets. We simply draped the sheets from the heads to figure out how to get a good body shape, and attached them to the bamboo sticks that supported the heads. Duct tape worked very well to firmly attach things. We used staples to attach the hands to the sheets.

Task 7: Movement rehearsal

Once the puppet was put together, we needed to practice how to move it. Students were put in teams for this so that they could rotate in and out and each have a turn to perform. The puppet needed to dance and gesture while a student narrator provided its voice. Each team rehearsed several times to perfect their movements (Figure 49).

Figure 49 Practising with a giant tree puppet.

Task 8: Dress rehearsal

We were able to run through the whole performance in advance, and get a sense of when and how to rotate puppeteers so everyone could be part of the performance (Figure 50).

Task 9: Performance!

The musical pageant to celebrate the 125th anniversary was a success.

Reflections, connections, and next directions

This project was tremendously meaningful to everyone involved. The puppet now resides at Sycamore Elementary School to help watch over and protect the students. It occasionally comes out to play.

Figure 50 Musical rehearsal for the pageant.

Figure 51 Sycamore Elementary students preparing for the puppet pageant.

Giant puppets are very popular with middle and high school populations (ages 12–18). They are also very good at writing performance texts for giant puppet pageants. I love helping these students discover the power of the chorus, which can provide powerful vocal and musical support. Musical instruments do not need to be fancy—never underestimate the power of dozens of kazoos.

If you find yourself in a position where you have to justify a project such as this, here (in fluent "academese") is a list of knowledge and skills students will gain from creating and presenting a giant puppet pageant.

Students will:

- Research and analyze multiple sources to identify possible symbols, metaphors, and historical information.

- Negotiate in groups to select one central image to construct as a giant puppet and gauge the effectiveness of design choices.

- Create props and dialogue that communicate clear ideas.

- Design and construct a giant puppet by creatively repurposing found materials.

- Revise text and movement to more effectively communicate, based on instructor and peer feedback

- Gain valuable experience with performance, building skills to improve performance under pressure (and handle testing situations more effectively).

THE FABULOUS ART OF PAPER MACHÉ

Version by Johanna

This technique is a combination of things I have learned from the Bread and Puppet Theatre, the Puppeteer's Cooperative, and my own experimentation in classrooms. I like it because it is really inexpensive, super safe and non-toxic, and models creative reuse.

Materials

- Old pot that you can use to boil at least a gallon/4 liters of water
- Cornstarch (one regular-sized household box makes more than enough for one day of work. For large projects I buy it in bulk)
- Several large containers for cool water
- Several plastic containers to hold the paste
- A large spoon or wire whisk
- Thick paper. Brown paper grocery bags with the handles and bottoms removed work very well
- Something to paper maché over, like a puppet head made of cardboard and newspaper.

Make the cornstarch paste in advance

Use a ratio of eight parts water to one part cornstarch. For example, if you measure 1 cup of cornstarch you will need 8 cups of water in total.

Take one measure of cornstarch and mix with one of your measures of water in one of your plastic containers. Stir until it behaves like thick milk. Feel free to add more water if you need to.

Take the rest of your water (seven measures or whatever is left) and boil it in a big pot.

Take the pot off the stove. While the water is very hot, stir it with your spoon or whisk while you drizzle in the cornstarch mixture. Keep stirring and adding the cornstarch mixture until it is a thick and gooey consistency.

Let the paste cool until it is safe to touch. It is really hot for a long time—be careful!

Prepare the paper

I have students help me rip paper grocery bags for this part. It is a fun stress reliever! They can also take unused paper to the recycling bin for you.

Remove the handles and bottoms of your paper bags. Rip the remaining pieces into smaller pieces. For small projects make them about the size of your hand. For larger ones they can be the size of notebook paper.

Dunk these pieces into your large containers of cool water. After a few minutes, wring out the excess water until the paper pieces are damp and pliable (like leather). You are doing this to break down the fibers in the paper and make it more flexible.

Spread a thin layer of paste on both sides of your prepared paper. I just dunk mine into a container of paste and scrape/squeeze off the excess. Use just a sheet at a time to keep it from drying out.

Applying the paper maché

Tear the glue-y paper into sizes that are small enough to lie flat over any curves. The tearing is important—the fibers that you can see at the edges are what holds the paper together so

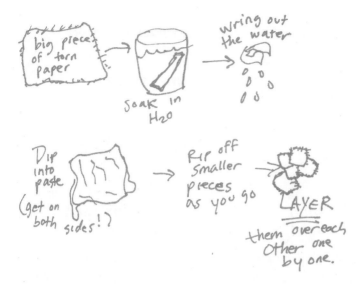

Figure 52 Paper maché how to.

strongly. I tend to tear as I go. As you lay the paper down on your puppet head, make sure to overlap the pieces. If a piece doesn't lie flat even after you smooth it, just remove it and try a smaller size. Each new piece should overlap about a third of the previous piece. This is what will give your paper maché a lot of strength.

When you finish one layer, let it dry before starting another layer. Most pieces need at least three layers. If you are using thinner paper you may need more.

A note on using clay molds

You can sculpt a puppet head out of clay, cover it with plastic wrap, and paper maché over that. When you are done you might need to carefully cut the paper with an exacto knife to remove it from the clay, but you can just paper maché over it later to fix it. You can reuse the clay mold to make multiple copies of a character.

You can usually reuse your clay if you keep it in an airtight container. You can also sculpt over an upturned plastic bowl or something similar if you don't have a lot of clay. Make sure the students understand the clay is not part of the puppet!

Using white glue like Elmer's glue to make paste

If, like most classrooms, you have access to a large amount of child-safe white glue, just pour some in a plastic container and thin it out with some water. Then prepare the paper as above.

Cleanup and keeping paste in between sessions

You can keep the paste between sessions if you cover it well. I always try to use recycled plastic containers with airtight lids (luckily most parents will happily gather these for you).

Cleanup should be easy—just use soap and water. It usually comes out of clothing. If you are worried, rinse it out quickly.

Finishing your puppet

You can paint your paper maché with any water-based, child-safe paint. After painting you may want to brush a layer of white glue over it to protect your paint job and seal it a bit. Attach hair, eyes, bodies, etc. using staples, glue, or any method that works for you.

Your puppet should last a very long time if it doesn't get wet.

12 Quick and Easy Ideas for Making Puppets

Introduction

This text is meant primarily for educators rather than professional puppet builders. There are wonderful resources for making professional-quality puppets which I strongly suggest you explore if you are interested. In particular, online puppet building tutorials are an incredible tool that I wish had been available when I was starting out. You can also learn to make puppets the old-fashioned way—by finding a puppet builder who is willing to show you some of their techniques and take you on as an "apprentice." Puppeteers in my life have been incredibly generous with their time and skills—it is a field that attracts some wonderful people. Somehow I have managed to acquire some fairly good skills thanks to their help.

However, I do have a particular expertise that may be useful that I am happy to share. After many years of working with children, I have found some tried-and-tested puppets that beginning puppeteers love to make. They also don't require any fancy tools or materials. You can make some of these to provide examples for sharing or use them as the basis for your own lessons and performances.

Finger puppets

All you need to make a finger puppet is a simple tube or sleeve that fits on your favorite finger. Use it as a base to attach things to and/or decorate. My favorite thing to use is a paper coin wrapper. Felt also makes a wonderful base for finger puppets. Younger children can simply glue shapes and features onto the base.

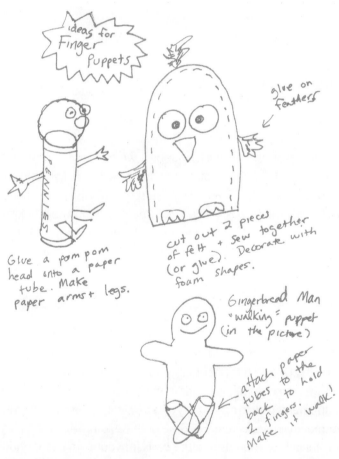

Figure 53 Finger puppet ideas.

Figure 54 Gingerbread man.

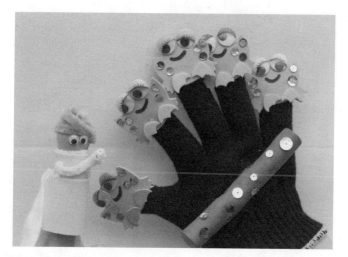

Figure 55 Finger and glove puppets.

Shadow puppets

I used a takeaway tin/lasagna pan to make this fish shadow puppet (Figures 57 and 58). The pieces are attached with wire. For paper shadow puppets see instructions in the shadow puppet lesson in Chapter 7.

Figure 56 Bees and rats puppets.

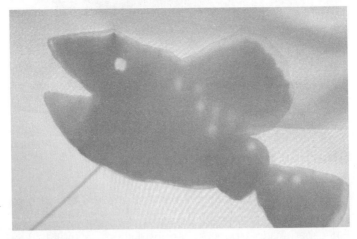

Figure 57 The front of a fish shadow puppet.

Figure 58 Back of the shadow puppet.

Two-dimensional (flat) puppets

Patterns photocopied onto cardstock are great to use in almost any lesson or story (see Coral Reef fish patterns in Chapter 9). Flat puppets are quick and easy as well as economical. Paper, cardboard, foam, cut out pictures from magazines, or even felt can be used to create a flat puppet. Simply glue your image on cardboard or cardstock, cut it out, and mount it on a craft stick or two. If you want, use a hole punch and brads to attach moving parts (just like shadow puppets but in full view). Make sure to decorate the front and back if the puppet needs to go in two directions, or simply make another one facing the opposite way or in a new position. If you need to make anything that has to be large, go with a flat puppet. You only need to make the part of the puppet that the audience sees—for example, a giant's legs and feet.

Hand puppets

Use newspaper and masking tape to create a puppet head shape over a cardboard tube that fits over your index and

Figure 59 Cow puppet.

Figure 60 Mouse and bug finger puppets.

middle fingers (together). Paper maché over it to make it strong (see instructions in Chapter 11). Paint and decorate it however you like. Use scrap fabric or even old clothing (sleeves from old shirts are wonderful) to make your puppet's body.

Anatomy of a hand puppet

You can also make them out of felt

Figure 61 Anatomy of a hand puppet.

Figure 62 Puppet of an old woman.

Simple folded paper puppets with moving mouths

Construction paper and glue sticks are all you need to make these guys. See Figure 63 for instructions on how to fold the paper base. Glue on paper legs and whatever else you like to create a character. The fact that they can move their mouths encourages children to create or repeat dialogue with their puppets. For example, these

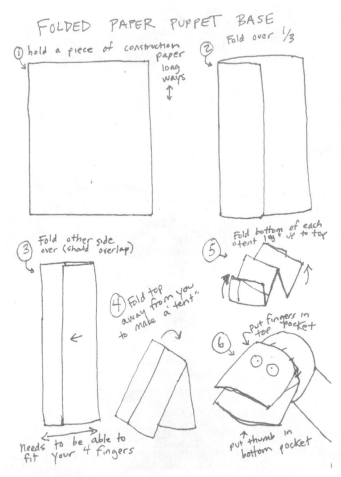

Figure 63 Folded paper puppet.

Figure 64 Folded paper puppet example.

are wonderful to use when interpreting frog and toad characters from stories. Students may need to practice synchronizing their mouth movements with their puppet. They should start by speaking slowly, and you should check to make sure they are opening the mouth of the puppet when the puppet is speaking. Many children naturally want to close their hand instead of open it because it feels more comfortable to them. Have them watch their hand and concentrate on that opening movement.

Sock puppets

Classic sock puppets are fun to use, easy to make, and also allow for mouth movement. Sometimes I create a more structured mouth for my sock puppets by gluing a folded cardboard circle into the sock, but that is not always necessary. Simply attach what you like on your sock using glue, staples, or a needle and thread. Don't wear the sock on your hand while using hot glue!

Figure 65 Sock and caterpillar puppets.

Glove puppets

Use hot glue to attach simple foam or felt characters onto the fingers of an inexpensive glove. Use it to sing a song or tell a little story to young children. I made one for the song "5 Green and Speckled Frogs" (see Figures 66 and 67). I can make them "jump" into a pool by wearing the glove backwards.

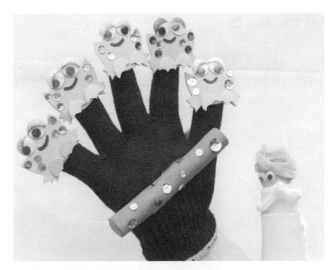

Figure 66 Frogs on the log—front of glove.

Figure 67 Frogs in pool—back of glove.

Rod puppets

All you need is a dowel or stick to start making a rod puppet. One-stick puppets can be very effective. I used a stuffed sock to make the dog in Figure 70, and the boy next to him is made out of a gourd that naturally included a "stick" as part of its shape. To make the puppets you see in Figure 69, use whatever method you like to make a head on one end of your stick. For one I used newspaper and tape and covered it in fabric, and for the other I found a cardboard box in the recycling and used it to make a head. Poke the center stick through the middle of a large circle of fabric and attach the puppet's neck to where you poked the hole. You can attach a hand to the fabric to make an arm (see Figure 68). Use another dowel, long chopstick, or coat hanger for the arm rod.

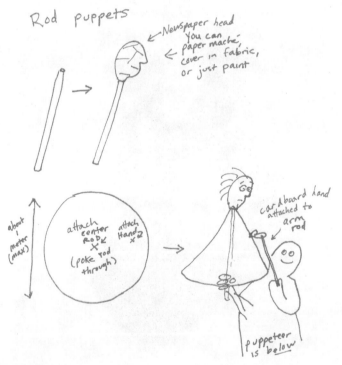

Figure 68 Rod puppet how to.

Figure 69 A couple of rod puppets in performance.

Figure 70 Boy and dog puppets.

"Junk" puppets

Don't forget that recycled stuff can make wonderful puppets and are especially useful for free-form puppet making. Use newspaper and tape to make all the characters in a story. Use a clean, empty container to make a rod puppet's head. Make your puppet's whole body out of a plastic bottle. The possibilities are endless! The rod puppet owl in Figure 71 was made out of a paper lunch bag.

Figure 71 Puppet of an owl.

Some other puppets types you can explore

Mouth/arm puppets

Children should be very familiar with these puppets, which are featured on screens around the world (Figures 72 and 73). They can have arms controlled by rods, or a puppeteer can use their own hand inside the puppet's "practical" hand. It is fun to have two puppeteers work one puppet. One person can be the head/moving mouth and one arm, while an assistant takes the other arm. Experiencing the collaboration necessary to do this is a lot of fun. If you are interested in learning how to make puppets like these, there are wonderful tutorials available online, or you can do what I did and learn from other puppeteers.

Figure 72 Blue mouth/arm puppet.

Figure 73 A beaver puppet inspired by Tina Turner.

Marionettes

Any puppet moved primarily by strings is technically a marionette. I love to make simple one-string versions in the classroom (I made the baby ducks in Figure 74 on one string so they could be used by toddlers). These puppets have an incredible history and can be sophisticated works of art that are difficult to master. Most puppeteers learn how to build and use them by working with a master puppeteer who specializes in marionettes. If you can, go to a professional marionette show, you won't believe your eyes.

Figure 74 Duck puppets.

Bun Raku (tabletop puppets with visible puppeteers)

Don't forget to remind students that puppets can be manipulated by more than one person, and one of the most comfortable ways to work is on a tabletop in full view of the audience. See the plastic bag puppet instructions in Chapter 3. This arrangement of puppeteers comes from the Japanese art form of Bun Raku. There is no way I can do this form justice, so please research this form of puppetry with your students. Any full body puppet form that you make could potentially be manipulated this way. You could even manipulate stuffed animals or dolls as puppet characters.

Ideas for puppet stages

- None (my favorite)
- Tabletop
- Folded screen

- Behind a table covered in a tablecloth—or even better turn the table on its side
- Cardboard box
- Sheet hung at kid height.

13 Finding Material for Puppetizing Lessons

How can I create my own Puppetizing lessons?

Now that we have explored some simple puppet-making ideas, I encourage you to apply these ideas to your own classroom material, whether it be children's literature, informational text, original stories, or even songs. Here are some questions I ask my students (who will soon be teachers in American public schools) to help them generate puppetry lessons and units.

1 **What material am I teaching?**

Here in California, we currently have to begin with the Standards as a starting point. We visit the Department of Education website and look over what California would like students to know and do at each grade level. In addition, California provides curriculum ideas and recommended literature. Our teachers have a lot of content to choose from. If you are a teaching artist, you might want to chat with your classroom partners to identify topics.

Example: Young students might be learning about life cycles in the natural world. The life cycle of a butterfly is a wonderful topic to explore through puppetry (in fact I will bet you are imagining caterpillar and butterfly puppets right now!).

2 Is there quality literature available for this material?

I am very fortunate to have access to a wonderful selection of children's literature in my University library. Our children's resource librarian takes care to order primarily award-winning books for our collection. Sometimes she has time to come to my class and share ways to find them. I take my students to the library and we look through the catalog and browse through the stacks of books to find possibilities. If you are currently teaching, you can look at your textbooks and think of how particular sections could be puppetized.

Example: There are several nonfiction books available that present a scientific overview of life cycles. You may also find fiction that accurately portrays a life cycle within the story. Make sure the terminology and factual information is correct before selecting a text.

3 If we consider everything a story, who are the characters in this material? What's the playable action?

Example: The life cycle of a butterfly needs to show one character changing through all of the stages of metamorphosis: egg, caterpillar, chrysalis, and adult butterfly. The focus of the action could be the transformation from one stage to another. Other important actions might be the caterpillar crawling and eating, and the butterfly flying.

4 How can I divide up the characters for puppet making? How can every child have a role in this story?

Example: It would be very possible to have each individual child in a class make all four stages of a butterfly's life cycle. If time is limited, you could simplify things and divide up the roles. For example, you could have half the class make caterpillars, and the other half butterflies, and provide fabric and pom poms to indicate eggs and chrysalises.

5 **What building approaches are my students developmentally prepared to explore?**

Example: Most students of school age are able to color a paper puppet pattern, cut it out, and glue it on a craft stick. As they are able to use more tools and materials, you can introduce more free-form or sophisticated building methods. Can they tie knots? Maybe they could use strings to manipulate their butterflies. Can they fold with accuracy? Maybe they could follow complicated directions or a demonstration for origami techniques to make butterfly wings. Can they solve problems independently or in small groups? Consider a free-form building approach and let them determine their own type of puppet.

6 **What kind of materials and tools do I have that my students are able to safely use?**

Often I will begin my process by seeing what's available, particularly when my budget is low.

Example: If I have a lot of cardboard tubes and construction paper and my students are too young to cut with detail, I may base my caterpillar puppet idea on gluing precut paper legs onto the tubes. If I have leftover tissue paper from decorating the classroom, I might use it for the butterfly wings.

7 **What is the best arrangement for puppetizing (using the puppets to bring the material to life)?**

Example: I could have students use their desks as a stage and guide all of the puppeteers through the puppetizing at once. That way if they are shy they will not feel like they're being put on the spot. I could have them perform their life cycle to a partner. I could put them in small groups and have them share short puppetizations behind a larger table. I could also use the whole room to move through the cycle together. We could start as egg puppets on one side, "hatch" into caterpillars and crawl a bit, pause to become chrysalises, and then emerge as adults, resulting in a flock of beautiful butterflies flying around the room.

Another tip

It can be very useful to take a look at the resources available for creative drama, theatre in education (TIE), and other forms of applied theatre methodologies for ideas that include (or can easily be modified to include) puppets. A lot of processes are very similar.

Here are some topics I have enjoyed exploring with puppetry. See if they inspire you too!

Science

Make molecule puppets and demonstrate the states of matter (solid, liquid, gas).

Create puppets to show the movement of Earth's continents over millions of years.

Make puppets of the planets and have them move through their orbits around a puppet sun.

Use a complex ecosystem as your topic and show how animals and plants interact, such as the Brazillian rain forest, African savanna, or Sonoran desert. See the coral reef lesson plan in Chapter 9 for inspiration.

Show evolution over long periods of time. Make puppets of dinosaurs from major eras and show them in their environments.

Show different kinds of weather and how creatures respond when it changes. Show how creatures behave when it is sunny, windy, rainy, or snowing.

Show how different peoples have adapted to life on Earth. Use people puppets to show how things such as housing, food, and clothing change based on the environment.

History

Use puppets to enact the building of the Egyptian pyramids.

Make puppet Viking ships and show where they explored.

Recreate the moon landing in your classroom.

Make puppets of famous leaders and have students recreate their most important speeches.

Math

Use animal puppets to add and subtract (birds in a nest, frogs on a log, etc.)

Make a puppet that is divisible by three (splits into three smaller creatures).

Make a "store" where animals have to add and subtract to buy things. Children can make their own puppets or use premade animals to become "customers."

Make puppet elves and have them measure and weigh holiday packages to ship to children.

Children's books

Certain types of children's literature lends itself to puppetizing. Here are some titles and topics that have worked for me.

Stories, rhymes, and songs that repeat

I Know an Old Person Who Swallowed a Fly

Stories with many characters

The Grouchy Ladybug

Why Mosquitoes Buzz in People's Ears

Hush! A Thai Lullaby

Who Said Moo?

The Gigantic Turnip

Myths and legends with cool animals and monsters (that are fun to turn into puppets and masks)

The Odyssey (Greece)

Anansi tales (Africa)

Coyote stories (Native American)

Reynard the Fox (France)

14 A Plan for Devising a New Puppet Play

Introduction

I believe in providing students with as many opportunities as possible to communicate clearly. This means that not only must performances and puppet designs be clearly understood by an audience, so must the story. In order to make sure they are understood as clearly as possible, students need to document what they do by writing it down. Puppetry can motivate students to write, especially because they do not follow traditional storytelling rules. Because they are so wonderfully weird, visual, and kinetic, they can inspire students who have difficulty writing.

I am a member of Generation X and I write how I was taught. I create a written outline (usually handwritten on a yellow legal pad) to provide an overall structure. Then I work to fill in the structure using all of my sources and supporting ideas. Then I revise (and revise and revise) before finally typing a final draft. This works well for me, but I have discovered that it is unfair of me to expect my students to write in the same way, especially if they are more fluent with visual communication (which seems to be the case more and more). It brings me comfort to realize that human communication hasn't changed so much that you and your students can't agree on how to tell a good story. *What* a good story is and *how* it should be documented may need to adjust with each generation. However, if students understand *why* it matters to communicate clearly for an audience, you have done the hard part—which is *motivating* the writing process.

Once you have a collection of puppet characters, it is incredibly fun to improvise with them and discover what they "want" to say and do. Then write down the dialogue and actions. Emphasize that the improvisation *is writing*! It is coming up with the ideas that will ultimately be on the written page. Sometimes we write the improvisations down like a play script, and sometimes we write only "beat sheets." These are a list of scenes and what happens in them (which is much more achievable for younger children). You can also add different kinds of writing, such as original poems for characters to say or sing.

I am comfortable with quite a bit of open-endedness for allowing students to find their own stories, but it can often be helpful to give them some specific structure to "hang" their story on. The following exercise has consistently generated good results for me.

The big question

How can we create a puppet play together using the structure of many myths and famous stories?

Materials

Whiteboard, chart paper or chalkboard for brainstorming, lots of paper and writing utensils, masking tape to hang things up, puppets for necessary characters (more on this later), a variety of materials such as cardboard, paint, etc. to create the performance environment.

Opening/hook

Ask students how many stories they can think of that have the following plot:

> *A hero is unsatisfied with their life and/or world and wishes they were someplace else. They are transported to a new place where all the rules are different. They are confronted by a villain (and their evil sidekicks if they have them). They are given a task of great difficulty to perform. They must go on a journey to complete this task, while the villain makes things even more challenging. Along the way they meet other characters who help them. They confront and defeat the villain. They realize what they have learned and are sent home with a new attitude.*

It should look familiar to them. This "Hero's Journey" is used by *The Wizard of Oz, Star Wars, The Neverending Story,* and many popular movies. It is also the structure for lots of fairy tales and myths! Inform students that they will be using this structure to create a new puppet play.

Task 1: Casting or creating the puppets

This activity is a wonderful opportunity to use store-bought or premade puppets, or puppets the students have recently created. Find all the puppet characters you have. Determine what kind of performance space would be best for the puppets available and how they will need to be performed. Remember, it is not always crucial to have a formal stage. If your puppeteers are visible that is just fine!

If you have the time and inclination, have students design and build their own puppets before starting the devising process.

I usually restrict the form the puppets should take based on what materials are available (for example, if I have access to lots of sticks, fabric, and coat hangers, they have to make simple rod puppets). Use whatever characters they come up with! This can be scary for some teachers, so I highly encourage you to keep it simple, or invite a professional puppeteer to help your students with the puppet making.

Decide which puppets will play the following characters by writing a cast list together. Also decide together what their character might be like based on their design.

- Hero (or heroes)
- The Hero's family or friends from daily life
- Creatures who live in the new world
- Villain (or villains)
- Evil sidekicks
- Helper characters.

Task 2: Map the story

There are many ways to organize the process of mapping the story, I usually draw a map on a big piece of paper and incorporate the students' input during a brainstorming session (Figure 75). The aim is to agree on the environment of the story and the kinds of things that will be around the characters. It is also useful to decide what the rules are in each "world."

Draw a map of two environments: "ordinary life," and the magical or strange land our hero visits. Draw the path of the journey our hero must take through the magical land (it should be a fairly circular path). Draw the magical creatures where they live. Then you will have a visual basis for the story before you write it. Keep it simple at first. Post the map where students can see it and encourage them to add things to it as they go along.

Figure 75 Story map.

Task 3: Improvised scenes

Assign students scenes to work on in groups. Make sure they understand the performance space and how they will need to manipulate their puppets. Locate where each scene takes place on the "story map." Make sure each group only does what they are assigned or it can get messy. Also encourage them to tell the story through actions and sounds as much as possible, and only have characters say what they need to say to be understood and nothing more. You may need to help the students decide who will play each character, but I have found that usually there are few issues. Some possible scenes are:

1 Hero interacts with family/friends at home.

2 Hero is magically transported to a new land, meets some creatures who live there, and discovers ways this new world is different.

3 Villain and sidekicks appear, confront the hero, and give them the difficult task. The first Helper could be one of the creatures who lives there. Helper 1 encourages the Hero and volunteers to go with them.

4 Hero and Helper 1 start on their journey and meet Helper 2 (it is useful to put each Helper in a specific environment of their own). Helper 2 should provide something they need. They decide to all go on together.

5 Hero and Helpers 1 and 2 continue on. The villain and sidekicks stop their progress by tricking them or putting up a barrier.

6 Helper 3 appears and provides what they need to fix the problem. The villain retreats. They all decide to go on together.

7 Hero and helpers reach their final destination. They solve part of their problem together.

8 The villain appears for a final showdown. The hero wins, of course! They defeat the villain however they want, which can also mean teaching them to be good from now on. The villain leaves.

9 Hero and helpers celebrate. They say goodbye to each other and the Hero goes home.

10 Hero tells his family/friends about his journey. He has changed in an important way.

Task 4: Share improvisations, revise, and write

Each group should share their scene. The audience should give them feedback and determine any new elements that should be added to the story map. After the scenes are as clear as possible, each group should write down the events/actions that happen. This is called a "beat sheet" and may look like this:

Scene 5

Villain tiptoes into the purple forest and laughs evilly.

Sidekicks enter, struggling to pull a giant net.

Villain orders sidekicks around as they set up a net as a trap in the trees.

Villain and sidekicks hear the hero coming and hide behind the trees.

Hero, Helper 1, and Helper 2 enter the purple forest and look around.

Helper 2 tells everyone they have a bad feeling about this place.

Scene 6

Helper 3 (a moving, talking purple tree) steps out of the forest and warns everyone about the net trap.

Helper 2 climbs Helper 3 to reach the net. They almost fall.

Helper 2 reaches the net and takes it down.

Villain and sidekicks appear and are mad.

Helpers chase away the villain and sidekicks.

It is also useful to mark down where any sound effects should happen. If students need to say a specific line, feel free to write it down on the beat sheet.

Task 5: Put it all together

Once all the beat sheets are completed, use them to guide rehearsals of the whole story. Usually I combine them into one typed document so it is easy to make changes and reprint revisions. I hang them up behind whatever stage we are using (along with the story map) so students can refer to them during their performance. This prevents a lot of stage fright issues! It will take a few rehearsals to get everything ready, but if you divide up the scenes it makes it easier to find the time to work with small groups. Invite an audience and put on your show.

Other things students can do for their puppet show

- Paint backdrops for each necessary environment and figure out how to hang them up
- Create props or necessary costume pieces
- Help "rig" the puppets with rods and strings so they can do the actions needed
- Design posters to advertise the show
- Create commercials for it to share over your school's announcement system
- Be the stage manager and make sure things are organized backstage
- Identify individual student strengths and find a way to incorporate them. I am always particularly happy to find student musicians and composers and put them to work on a theme song to play for each character when they appear.

Conclusion

As part of my recent Puppetry in the Classroom course at my university, I invited preschoolers from the University Childcare Center to come join us for "tiny little puppet shows." Each of my preservice teaching students had prepared a "glove" or "finger" puppet to tell a memorized story. We divided into groups and divided the children into four "audiences" so they would see about fifteen minutes of puppet shows (which ended up being very appreciated by their teachers as they would not have enjoyed sitting much longer).

I don't think it would be possible for me to be more pleased not only by the reactions of the children but by the excitement and passion of my own students after experiencing the power of puppets. They were surprised and delighted by how the children were completely riveted by the simplest techniques. After the stories, the children were invited to try the puppets themselves, and almost all of them immediately chose a character, put it on their finger, and began moving it while speaking in their voice. My students felt that this was the most incredible part of the activity. The children were joyfully playing while experimenting with language, communication, emotion, comprehension, and storytelling. My students felt empowered and inspired by how simple and effective their work had been, and for me that was incredibly rewarding.

Teachers can be apprehensive about competing with all the stories children see on screens. What many educators don't

Figure 76 My puppetry student experiencing magic with a five-year-old friend.

realize is that puppets occupy a completely different space for children. They are *real*. They can be touched, interacted with, heard—and yet they are beyond ordinary life. Children will say things to a puppet and through a puppet that they would never say to a human. It would be so simple and easy for all teachers everywhere to use puppets to teach children empathy, kindness, and a fearless love of learning. I invite my readers to share their experiences and discoveries with others so we can spread "puppet power" around the world. Let's convince policy makers that we should make it part of every child's life. Our best argument is our direct experience.

Bibliography

Baird, Bill and Arie De Zanger (illus.). *The Art of the Puppet*. New York: Macmillan, 1965.

Hough, Brian and Sigmund Hough. "The Play Was Always the Thing: Drama's Effect on Brain Function." *Psychology*, vol. 3 no. 6, 2012, 454–456.

Hunt, Tamara and Nancy Renfro. *Puppetry in Early Childhood Education*. Austin, TX: Nancy Renfro Studios, 1982.

Jurkowski, Henryk. *Aspects of Puppet Theatre*, 2nd ed. Basingstoke: Palgrave Macmillan, 1988.

Marshall, Julia. "Transdisciplinarity and Art Integration: Toward a New Understanding of Art-based Learning Across the Curriculum." *Studies in Art Education*, vol. 55 no. 2, 2014, 104–127.

Miranda, Anne. *Fishy Fact*. New York: Macmillan/McGraw-Hill, 1997.

Tillis, Steve. "The Actor Occluded: Puppet Theatre and Acting Theory." *Theatre Topics*, vol. 6 no. 2, 1996, 109–119. *Project MUSE*, doi:10.1353/tt.1997.0014.

Wiggins, Grant P. and Jay McTighe. *Understanding by Design*, expanded 2nd ed. Alexandria, VA: Association for Supervision and Curriculum Development, 2005.

Wilson, Frank R. *The Hand: How Its Use Shapes the Brain, Language, and Human Culture*. New York: Vintage Books, 1999.

Wilson, Margaret. "Six Views of Embodied Cognition." *Psychonomic Bulletin & Review*, vol. 9 no. 4, 2002, 625–636.

Recommended resources for puppetry education

Many of these authors have multiple titles that are all quite good.

Bernier, Matthew and Judith O'Hare. *Puppetry in Education and Therapy: Unlocking Doors to the Mind and Heart*. Bloomington, IN: Authorhouse, 2005.

Crepeau, Ingrid M. and M. Ann Richards. *A Show of Hands: Using Puppets with Young Children*. St. Paul, MN: Red Leaf Press, 2003.

Currell, David. *Puppets and Puppet Theatre*. Wiltshire: Crowood Press, 2015.

Henson, Cheryl, David Cain, and John E. Barrett. *The Muppets Make Puppets: How to Make Puppets out of All Kinds of Stuff around Your House*. New York: Workman Pub, 1994.

Hunt, Tamara and Nancy Renfro. *Puppetry in Early Childhood Education*. Austin, TX: Nancy Renfro Studios,1982.

Kennedy, John E. *Puppet Mania!*. Cincinnati, OH: North Light Books, 2004.

Latshaw, George. *The Complete Book of Puppetry*. New York: Dover Press, 2000.

Other titles

Spolin, Viola. *Improvisation for the Theater*. Evanston: IL: Northwestern University Press, 1999.

Index